GUTS & GLORY

The American Civil War

GUTS & GLORY

The American Civil War

BEN THOMPSON

ILLUSTRATIONS BY
C. M. BUTZER

Little, Brown and Company

New York   Boston

Little, Brown and Company

Hachette Book Group
1290 Avenue of the Americas, New York, NY 10104
Visit us at lb-kids.com

Little, Brown and Company is a division of Hachette Book Group, Inc.
The Little, Brown name and logo are trademarks of Hachette Book Group, Inc.

The publisher is not responsible for websites (or their content) that are not owned by the publisher.

First Edition: October 2014

Library of Congress Cataloging-in-Publication Data

Thompson, Ben.
Guts & glory : the American Civil War / by Ben Thompson; illustrations by C. M. Butzer — First edition.
pages cm
Includes bibliographical references and index.
ISBN 978-0-316-32050-4 (hardcover) — ISBN 978-0-316-32053-5 (ebook) — ISBN 978-0-316-32197-6 (library edition ebook)   1. United States—History—Civil War, 1861–1865—Juvenile literature. 2. United States—History—Civil War, 1861–1865—Campaigns—Juvenile literature. I. Butzer, C. M., illustrator.   II. Title.   III. Title: Guts and glory.
E468.T48 2014
973.7—dc23
2013041699

10 9 8 7 6 5 4 3 2 1

RRD-C

Book design by Tom Daly

Printed in the United States of America

Special thanks to the Civil War Institute at Gettysburg College

Image Credits:
Courtesy of the Naval Historical Foundation: page 167
Courtesy of the US Library of Congress: pages 8, 23, 26, 36, 108, 120, 152, 186, 281, 294

We'll fight them, sir, 'til hell freezes over. And then, sir, we will fight them on the ice.

—Anonymous soldier at the Battle of Gettysburg

Contents

> This country will be drenched in blood, and God only knows how it will end.
>
> —Major General William Tecumseh Sherman, US Army

A 275-pound mercenary captain leads more than four hundred knife-swinging Louisiana ex-cons screaming into battle, kicking off the Civil War with an epic, full-throttle charge straight into the teeth of the advancing Union army.

Looking to break out of a Union naval blockade that holds the Southern economy in a stranglehold, the Rebels build a gigantic steam-powered metal warship and ram it into every old-school wooden vessel in sight.

7. The Deadliest Day 95

Lee's army takes the fight to the Union, marching out of Virginia in a full-scale assault on the North, and finds itself in a bare-knuckled street brawl that will result in more deaths than any other single-day battle in American history.

8. Chancellorsville 109

Outnumbered two to one in the impenetrable wilderness of Northern Virginia, the now legendary general Stonewall Jackson leads his battle-hardened veterans on an all-or-nothing gamble to turn the tables against the Union.

9. Horse and Steel 121

In the largest cavalry battle ever to take place on North American soil, the intense sword fights and close-quarters combat of the Battle of Brandy Station were more akin to a medieval beatdown than a modern industrial war.

10. Gettysburg 134

The Confederacy reaches its high-water mark in the largest and most important battle to ever take place on American soil. When the smoke finally clears, the course of American history will be changed forever.

15. The Rock of Chickamauga

With his allies in full retreat and his embattled command hammered on three sides by the full might of the Confederate army, the fate of the Union army suddenly rests in the hands of a Virginian.

16. Union Nurse

Working in miserable conditions amputating limbs during the critical Battle of Chattanooga, the only female surgeon of the war would become the first—and to this day only—woman ever to receive the Medal of Honor.

17. Grant Versus Lee

Get ready for the final, inevitable, life-or-death showdown between two of the greatest and most revered generals in US history.

18. Mobile Bay

Seeking to cut off the final bastion for Rebel blockade runners, the first admiral of the US Navy straps himself to the mast of his ship and steams right into a fortified Confederate stronghold.

Introduction

✪ ✪ ✪

> The Civil War defined us as what we are and it opened us to
> being what we became, good and bad things....It was the
> crossroads of our being, and it was a hell of a crossroads.
>
> —Shelby Foote, *The Civil War: A Narrative*

WITH HIS TEETH CLENCHED AND HIS EYES
resolutely fixed on the imposing walls of the Confederate fort looming in front of him, Color Sergeant Alexander
Campbell of the Seventy-Ninth New York Volunteer Infantry
gripped a heavy, nine-foot-tall wooden staff proudly bearing
the flag of the United States of America and raced ahead as
fast as his legs could carry him, charging through the humid,
sun-drenched swamplands of Secessionville, South Carolina,
toward the enemy. Somehow ignoring the hail of bullets ripping
past his head, Campbell bravely led a sea of blue-coated Union
soldiers hurtling through the ankle-deep marsh, their rifled

muskets brandishing steel bayonets that glinted menacingly in the sunlight. Even as many of his comrades fell around him, Campbell forged ahead. When he reached the wooden walls of the Rebel fort, Campbell clambered his way up, slugged a defender with a crushing blow from his staff, and planted the bullet-riddled Stars and Stripes on the parapet, screaming for his men to follow him.

Atop the walls, the Confederate defenders of Secessionville rushed to counter the Union breach, battling the Federal onslaught with everything they had available. One fearsome warrior from the First South Carolina Infantry Battalion already had his weapon obliterated by an enemy bullet, but this wasn't about to stop him. He ran up to the parapet, saw a group of Federals charging toward him, and shoved a big log off the ledge, knocking the Yankees back into the swampland below. Suddenly attacked by another Union trooper at the top of the wall, the now unarmed Rebel dodged a bayonet thrust, grabbed his opponent's rifle, ripped it from his hands, and shot him with his own gun.

This Confederate soldier's name was James Campbell. He was Union flag bearer Alexander Campbell's big brother. Two men, related by blood, fighting a life-or-death struggle on opposite sides of the same battle.

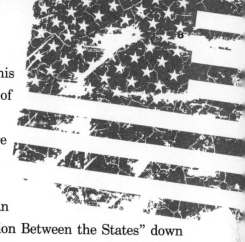

How does something like this happen? In the United States, of all places?

Countless volumes and entire chapters of boring textbooks have been devoted to describing the causes of the "American Civil War of Northern Aggression Between the States" down to every single nauseating detail from a day-by-day re-creation of Bleeding Kansas to a description of the type of underwear Abraham Lincoln was wearing at his presidential inauguration ceremony. The short answer is that the war was fought over slavery, but that doesn't quite cover it. In actuality, the vast majority of Confederate troops fought for the South even though they never owned a single slave, and many Union soldiers were ultra-passionate about enlisting and fighting for their cause even though the institution of slavery wasn't formally abolished in the United States until after the war had already been going on for almost three years.

So what the heck was this all about, then?

To say that the events leading up to the presidential election of 1860 were pretty intense would be like saying that swan-diving into an active volcano is kind of a bad idea. Basically, the United States at this time was about as divided as you could get. In the South, wealthy plantation owners utilized millions of black slaves, many of whom were kept under incredibly harsh, unforgivably barbaric conditions, to harvest their tobacco and cotton crops, which were then shipped to the ultra-industrial North for massive profit. The Southern elite were constantly worried that some uppity Yankee politician was going to deprive them of their so-called "right" to exploit free labor for profit, so they made it their mission to expand slavery into the territory the United States gained after its war with Mexico as a means of protecting their plantations. The industrial Northern states, which had already outlawed slavery as cruel and unusual punishment, naturally tried to block this at all costs. The results were intense political tension, a handful of gunfights in border towns, and a whole lot of bad blood between North and South.

All this came to a head in the presidential election of 1860, when the ardently antislavery Republican candidate, Abraham Lincoln, defeated Democrat Stephen A. Douglas and a couple of other dudes and was elected the sixteenth president of the United States. Lincoln, who was so hated in the South that he didn't even appear on the ballot in ten states, swept the Northern electoral vote, ultimately receiving 39.8 percent of the national popular vote, and was elected to office.

This was the last straw for the South. Seven states seceded from the Union immediately, forming the Confederate States of America. They seized US forts and arsenals, created their own government, and elected Mississippi senator Jefferson Davis to serve as their president.

This move set the United States spiraling into a firestorm that would rip the country in half and lead to the bloodiest war in American history. Lincoln, determined to keep the Union together, put out a call for volunteers to fight and defend America from these dangerous Rebels who would dare to break it apart. Union newspapers declared death to the traitors, and all across the North, patriots rallied to the Stars and Stripes, eager to preserve the United States as one country, indivisible, with liberty and justice for all.

Well, this call to arms wasn't heeded as well in some of the Southern states, many of which weren't down with fighting a war against their fellow Southerners. As the North prepared for war, four more states refused to raise arms for the Union and seceded, their governments putting out a similar request for men to come to the aid of the South. Southerners—many of them poor farmers who never owned slaves themselves but whose loyalty lay with their home state and not the Federal government—flocked to the Confederate banner and prepared to do battle with an army they perceived as an invading force seeking to unconstitutionally impose its will on the South.

The battle lines had been drawn—twenty-one heavily populated Northern industrial states against eleven rural Southern states. The Union had the manpower, industry, railroads, and infrastructure to outnumber and outproduce the agrarian South, but they would be fighting on enemy soil against a determined foe. The Confederacy had the advantage of fighting on their home turf against an invading army, and had much more experienced generals. They also still held out hope that the great European powers—England and France, both of which depended very heavily on Southern cotton exports to keep their economies running—might come to their aid and help them defeat the US forces and preserve their newfound independence.

The first shots of the Civil War were fired on April 12, 1861, when South Carolina coastal artillery batteries shelled the Union garrison at Fort Sumter, off the coast of Charleston. The Confederates bombed the fort for about a day and a half before it surrendered, the only fatalities being two Union dudes who accidentally blew themselves up after the battle was already over, but everyone got the point and they were pretty much just pumped up that it was finally time to stop talking and start fighting.

The stage was now set for a war that would pit brother against brother and tear the entire country apart.

What happened next would claim more lives than every previous American war combined and redefine the United States of America forever.

Population

US: 18.5 million

CS: 5.5 million, plus 3.5 million slaves

Border: 2.5 million, plus 500,000 slaves

Enlistment

US: 2.67 million • CS: 1 million

Industry

US: 101,000 factories, 1.1 million workers,
20,000 miles of railroad

CS: 21,000 factories, 111,000 workers,
9,000 miles of railroad

US = United States

CS = Confederate States

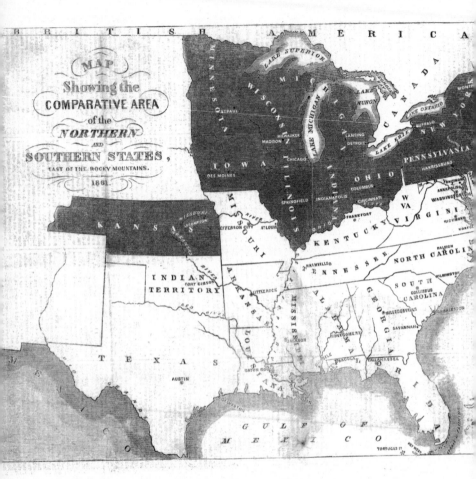

The Union included the states of Maine, New York, New Hampshire,
Vermont, Massachusetts, Connecticut, Rhode Island, Pennsylvania,
New Jersey, Ohio, Indiana, Illinois, Kansas, Michigan, Wisconsin,
Minnesota, Indiana, California, and Oregon. Abraham Lincoln was
their president. West Virginia and Nevada became states during the
course of the Civil War (West Virginia was specifically formed from
a portion of Virginia that opted not to secede) and entered on the
side of the Union.

Major American Conflicts Through 1865

War	Opponent	Estimated US Casualties
American Revolution (1775–1783)	Great Britain	33,769 [1]
War of 1812 (1812–1815)	Great Britain	6,765 [2]
Second Seminole War (1835–1842)	Seminole Indians	1,500 [3]
Mexican-American War (1846–1848)	Mexico	17,435
Civil War (1861–1865)	——	1,500,000 [4]

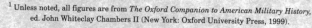

[1] Unless noted, all figures are from *The Oxford Companion to American Military History*, ed. John Whiteclay Chambers II (New York: Oxford University Press, 1999).

[2] Figure includes battle dead and wounded only. If deaths from disease and attrition were included, the number would likely be noticeably higher.

[3] From the *Encyclopedia of American Indian Wars: 1492–1890*, ed. Jerry Keenan (New York: W. W. Norton, 1999).

[4] Most recent modern estimates of Union and Confederate army casualties combined.

Author's Note

★ ★ ★

THE CIVIL WAR IS IN MY BLOOD. I HAVE EIGHT ancestors on my father's side alone who served with Robert E. Lee in the Army of Northern Virginia, all of them rural, non-slaveholding Virginia farm boys. Of these eight, all of whom enlisted in time to serve in the Battle of First Manassas, three didn't return after setting out on Pickett's Charge at the Battle of Gettysburg; three more were taken prisoner at Sayler's Creek, and, of those three, one died in prison two months after the war was already over. One was pardoned at Appomattox (his discharge paperwork hangs in my living room); the other was wounded in the head and hand at Gettysburg and didn't make it back into action until the end of the war. My mother's side claims some tangential descent from Joseph E. Johnston that I've never been able to document, but the war is embedded in my genetic code on that side too—my mother's family farm is a landmark on maps of the Battle of Sayler's Creek and is visible in photographs of the battlefield from 1865.

I have studied the Civil War intensely all my life, and in my fifteen years off and on as a Civil War reenactor wearing both Confederate gray and Union blue, I've fought as part of Wheat's Tigers, Forrest's Cavalry, Sheridan's Raiders, and the Army of Northern Virginia, been killed in Pickett's Charge twice, engaged in hand-to-hand combat with Sherman's troops at Resaca, been blown up charging Confederate artillery alongside the Fifty-Fourth Massachusetts at the Battle of Olustee, and—I kid you not—had a full-blooded Seminole Indian run up out of nowhere and whack me in the head with a rubber tomahawk in front of hundreds of spectators.

This stuff is what I live for.

As a man who has the South in his veins but also loves the United States of America with all his heart, I can understand exactly why men of both sides would fight and die for their respective causes in this war. As such, in writing this book I have attempted to present courageous heroes and cowardly villains from both sides equally, showing each in their full glory without trying to pull any punches whatsoever. In each chapter I have attempted to pick a point of view and run with it full-throttle, concerning myself primarily with highlighting *why* these men and women fought and *what* exactly they accomplished, rather than attempting to inject some annoying political statement or any of that garbage. These are the stories. I encourage you to dig deeper, read the primary sources, and draw your own conclusions.

These stories are presented in chronological order, from the war's first battle to its last. Rather than settling on just the "greatest hits," I've tried to find a good mix of different people, battles, and events, each with their own feel and flavor, to show exactly how diverse this war could be, and tie them all together into a narrative that brings the reader along for the ups and downs of the darkest, bloodiest, and most defining moment in American history.

First Blood

The First Battle of Bull Run (First Manassas)

July 21, 1861 ✻ Manassas, Virginia

> Our blood was on fire. Life was valueless. The boys fired one volley, then rushed upon the foe with clubbed rifles beating down their guard; then they closed upon them with their knives, "Greek had met Greek," the tug of war had come.... [It] did not seem as though men were fighting... [but as if there] were devils mingling in the conflict, cursing, yelling, cutting, and shrieking.
>
> —Private Robert Richie, First Louisiana Special Battalion

ON THE MORNING OF JULY 21, 1861, THE Union army had one thing and one thing only on its mind—the complete destruction of all Southern forces and a permanent end to the Rebellion. With a battle cry of "Forward to Richmond!" thirty-five thousand tough-as-nails volunteer soldiers of the US Army marched to the battlefield at Manassas Junction, Virginia, a mere twenty miles from Washington, DC, seeking an epic one-day showdown that would determine the fate of the country forever. Arrayed against them were a mere twenty thousand Southerners—a ragtag band of rebellious farm boys who certainly couldn't stand toe-to-toe with the full might of the US military. If they could crush this motley assortment of traitors like bugs, nothing stood between the Federal army and the Confederate capital of Richmond, Virginia, and a quick end to the Civil War.

The Union had the manpower. They had the weapons and equipment. And they were on the offensive. They were so confident of victory that regular folks from the North packed picnic baskets and walked along behind the Union army so that they could eat lunch and have some pleasant conversation with their friends while they watched the Rebellion stamped out before them in one simple afternoon of work.

Even though he knew most soldiers on both sides were fighting in their first battle, the Northern commander, General Irvin McDowell, had a plan that would almost certainly catch the Rebels with their pants down. He'd deployed most of his army along the banks of Bull Run Creek, the river that surrounded the train depot at Manassas Junction, right next to a large stone bridge. The Confederates, looking for any advantage they could get, lined up all their guys on the opposite side of the bridge so they could shoot at the Union when they tried to cross.

Except the Union didn't try to cross there. Instead, they took twenty thousand of their men, snuck them through the woods, crossed Bull Run Creek a mile upstream without the Confederates realizing it, and then came running out of the forest from the side the Rebels least expected it, hollering in New England accents and waving their bayonets around like they meant it.

It was a brilliant plan. Or it would have been, if it hadn't been for one thing: They ran into the First Louisiana Special Battalion—the most infamous unit in the Confederate army.

Recruited in the seediest prisons and docks of New Orleans by a Rebel army desperate for manpower, the 415 criminals, thieves, and wharf rats of the First Louisiana Special Battalion had arrived at Manassas Junction a few weeks earlier. When they'd shown up, many of them had to be carried off the train because they'd been bound and gagged during the ride because of disorderly conduct. The First then proceeded to start a drunken brawl in Lynchburg, Virginia, fistfight a company from the Twenty-First Georgia Infantry in a dispute over a stolen whiskey bottle, and then storm the Confederate stockade with torches and muskets in the middle of the night to break out a couple of their men who had been arrested and were awaiting their court-martials.

Oh yeah, and every man in the unit was packing a twelve-inch bowie knife that basically resembled a hillbilly machete.

As the Union troops approached, the First Louisiana drew
their knives, waved them over their heads, growled like animals, and chanted, "Gumbo, gumbo, Yankee gumbo!"

Under the command of thirty-five-year-old Major Cha-
tham Roberdeau Wheat, a gigantic, six-foot-four, 275-pound,
larger-than-life professional mercenary with sixteen years
of experience fighting in Cuba, Mexico, Nicaragua, Italy,
and a half-dozen other places across the world, this unit of
knife-wielding convicts (appropriately nicknamed Wheat's
Tigers) wasn't about to turn around and run home crying to
their prison cells just because they were being attacked by a
force that outnumbered them about a hundred to one. They
were going to hold the line as long as it would possibly take
for the Rebels to reorganize and prepare their defenses.

The first troops up were 5,500 men
from the Seventy-First New York
and the Second Rhode Island,
two full-strength regiments
of volunteer infantry under
the command of General
Ambrose Burnside. Burn-
side, a former tailor whose
facial hair was so intense
that the word *sideburns*
was created to describe his
glorious muttonchops, ordered

his men to charge up Matthew's Hill, destroy the Tigers, turn the Confederate flank, and end this war with one glorious attack that would be told by history books forever. Behind him were thirteen thousand Federal troops who had no intention of stopping until they'd torn the Rebel flag off the Confederate capitol building in Richmond and thrown it into a pit of red-hot magma.

Major Wheat calmly ordered his rowdy Tigers to fall back to the reverse slope of Matthew's Hill, find some cover, and prepare for the fight of their lives.

The moment that the Union troops arrived on the summit of the hill, the Tigers unleashed a huge volley that rocked the Federal lines. The Union soldiers, still trying to bring their artillery up to the battlefront, returned fire as best they could, but they were easy targets at the top of the hill as they shot down at men who were hidden behind cover.

For the next hour the two sides exchanged gunfire, hurling bullets into a fog of gun smoke that limited visibility to about fifty yards, as Wheat's Tigers somehow managed to hold back a full brigade of Burnside's troops for a ridiculous amount of time, considering how lopsided the numbers were. Their courageous struggle bought time for the rest of the Confederate forces to redeploy in a defensive position along Henry House Hill—the next ridge behind Matthew's Hill—but before long things were starting to look bad for the Tigers. The Rhode Islanders had brought up the full might of their artillery, and as cannonballs rained onto Wheat's forces, they started taking heavy casualties.

Then, suddenly, an earth-churning cannonball explosion sent a huge chunk of shrapnel ripping through Major Wheat's lungs, taking the big man to the ground with a sickening thud. His men, confident that they'd held the line as long as they possibly could, wrapped their commander in the unit's flag and started to fall back toward Henry House Hill. When he was examined by a doctor moments later, the medic somberly informed Wheat that "there is no instance on record of recovery from this type of wound." Wheat responded, "Then I will put my case on record....I don't feel like dying just yet."

He lived. He'd even see the battlefield once again but would be mortally wounded at Gaines' Mill a year later.

Now, in most cases, this would be the end of the story. Wheat's Tigers put up a great fight, gave the Yankees everything they had, held off the enemy's varsity team for over an hour, and now, thanks to the loss of their commanding officer, were in full retreat.

As they approached Henry House Hill, however, the Tigers saw something that changed their minds and renewed their will to fight.

Standing defiantly atop the hill was General Thomas J. Jackson, a professor of philosophy and artillery tactics at the Virginia Military Institute. Jackson had moved to this position while the Tigers held back Burnside's men, and now he stood there in the midst of all the chaos around him, ordering his assembled Virginia regiments to open fire on anything in a blue uniform.

It was at this point that one Confederate general shouted, "There stands Jackson like a stone wall! Rally around the Virginians!"

From that point on, Jackson would be known by the incredibly awesome-sounding nickname Stonewall Jackson. This won't be the last you'll hear of him.

The Tigers, inspired by Jackson's bravery and still eager for Yankee blood, fell in line with the Virginians atop Henry House Hill and continued their fight. The Union forces under Burnside pressed on, eager to take the hill and complete their virulent assault on the Confederate flank, but Stonewall refused to give an inch of ground, his men blasting at the "blue bellies" with everything in their arsenal despite having their lines brutally hammered by Union infantry and cannons. The stouthearted stand of Stonewall and the Tigers stopped the Union attack in its tracks.

Then, out of nowhere, Jackson ordered his men to do the one thing the Union least expected.

Charge.

With a loud, terrifying, earsplitting shriek that would soon be infamously known as the "Rebel yell," the Fourth and Thirty-Third Virginia Infantry Regiments charged ahead, bayonets at the ready. Upon seeing this, Captain Alex White, the acting commander of Wheat's Tigers now that Wheat himself was wounded, ordered his already exhausted men to follow suit and charge the Union artillery positions. White was struck by a bullet almost immediately upon leading the attack, but as he lay there bleeding he shouted something I'm not allowed to print here, but that basically amounts to "They'll never take us alive, boys—go get 'em!"

The four-hundred-something surviving men of Wheat's Tigers grabbed their rifles and charged the Union lines. When they got close enough, they drew their bowie knives and hurled themselves at the Federal troops, hacking and stabbing with knives and swinging their rifles like baseball bats.

The bold attack was a raging success. The Confederates captured the Union artillery positions, turned the Yankee cannons around, and fired double loads of canister shot point-blank into the Union infantry, blasting their front lines with a shotgun shell of cannonballs. It wasn't long before the Union army was in full retreat, knocking over the civilian spectators and stepping on their picnic baskets as they hurried back to Washington.

The first major battle of the Civil War had ended. And it was becoming increasingly obvious to all parties involved that this war wasn't going to be over as quickly as everyone had expected.

Rose O'Neal Greenhow

Rebel troops were alerted to the Union attack at Manassas by one of their most important spies: a wealthy high-society woman living in Washington, DC, named Rose O'Neal Greenhow. Greenhow lived in a sweet house and would throw awesome parties, then get all the generals' wives drunk and ask them for good gossip about the war. She'd then use a complicated cipher to encrypt the messages, and a network of couriers would deliver the info to Confederate lines. Greenhow kept this up even after being placed under house arrest in 1862, so the Union threw her in prison, where she continued to write notes and send them to the South. Eventually they figured, forget it, released her, and shipped her off to live in the South, since she apparently liked it so much there.

Battle Names

One of the confusing/annoying things about the Civil War is that the North and the South had different names for some of the same battles. Basically, the North would name battles after the closest river, and the South would name them after the closest city. So the Battle of Manassas in the South is known as the Battle of Bull Run in the North.

The War Before the Civil War

Most Civil War unit commanders were already veterans who had gained valuable experience fighting in the Mexican-American War from 1846 to 1848. Back then, Mexico used to be way huger than it is now, and the United States wanted a piece of it, so not long after Texas seceded from Mexico in the Texas Revolution (this is where that whole "Remember the Alamo" thing comes from), the United States went to Mexico and was like, "Hey, we'll give you thirty million dollars if you give us all your territory north of the Rio Grande." When the Mexicans said no, the Americans marched troops into their land and started blowing things up. The Americans demolished the Mexicans, captured Veracruz, and marched all the way into Mexico City. The ensuing peace treaty granted the United States 525,000 miles of new territory, which became the states of California, Nevada, Utah, Arizona, New Mexico, Wyoming, and Colorado. Whether or not these new territories would come into the Union as free states or slave states was a key source of tension between North and South, and is one of the major causes of the Civil War.

Landing of the American forces under General Winfield Scott at Veracruz, March 9, 1847

The First Battle of Bull Run (First Manassas)

Troops
Union: 28,450

Confederate: 32,230

Casualties
Union: 2,896

Confederate: 1,982

Result
Confederate Victory

The Battle Line

Nineteenth-century warfare was very, very different from the way modern wars are fought. There was very little hiding behind cover, no circle-strafing, and no calling in air strikes from military drones or AC-130s....This was man against man, face-to-face, hardcore stuff—old-school-style warfare with guns. Instead of taking cover and spreading out and hiding behind things like some kind of wimp, real men would stand side by side, shoulder to shoulder, in two ranks, and when their commander shouted "Forward, march!" they'd stand tall and walk straight ahead into enemy bullets and cannon fire.

This was mostly still a throwback to the days of bow-and-arrow archers and old-school, single-shot muskets that were about as accurate on the battlefield as a rubber-band gun—the only way to hit what you were aiming at was to put a bunch of rifles in a really small space, fire, hope you hit something, then keep marching until you were close enough so that you could stab the enemy with a bayonet (a nasty-looking device that looks like a sword that attaches to the end of a gun). Eighteenth-century muskets shot once, took twenty-five seconds to reload, fired a .69-caliber solid circular musket ball, and were deadly accurate out to about fifty yards.

The .58-caliber minié ball, invented by French Army captain Claude-Étienne Minié in 1848, changed all that by making rifled musket ammunition cheap and reliable. In the hands of a trained rifleman, this hollow-point, conical "minnie bullet" could kill at 1,200 yards, and the new percussion cap system made it so it could be reloaded in about twenty seconds and would still shoot in the rain.

Commanders still tried to use bayonet charges to attack minié ball–equipped riflemen, and, let's be honest, it was much better to test your foot speed crossing fifty yards in twenty-five seconds than it is pushing your luck trying to run two and a half football fields in twenty seconds.

Obviously, lining up and walking to your death is a pretty terrible idea under these conditions, but that's the way wars had been fought for thousands of years, and most Civil War commanders weren't about to change that. The result is one of the reasons why this was the deadliest war in American history.

Old Stone House, Manassas Battlefield, Manassas, Virginia

A Clash of Ironclads

The *Monitor* and the *Merrimack*

Hampton Roads, Virginia ∗ *March 8–9, 1862*

> The combat of the *Merrimac* and the *Monitor*
> made the greatest change in sea-fighting
> since cannon fired by gunpowder had
> been mounted on ships.
>
> —Winston Churchill, British prime minister 1940–1945

SEEING AS HOW THE UNION'S SEMI-BRILLIANT plan of "Hey, dudes, let's just charge straight at them full-frontal-assault-style and see what happens" didn't work out quite as well as they were hoping, the North decided, forget that, let's try something way more overly complicated instead. Under the direction of new overall army commander George McClellan, the Yankees adopted a new plan—they'd leave a huge force behind to protect Washington, DC, and keep the Confederates occupied, and meanwhile they'd sail down the Atlantic coast, drop a few hundred thousand dudes behind enemy lines on the peninsula outside Yorktown, Virginia, then go around and attack Richmond from the back. The Confederates didn't have nearly enough soldiers to defend their capital from both sides at the same time, so this one-two punch to the neck and kidneys would almost certainly be the thing to break the pesky Rebellion's back once and for all.

The first stage of the Northern assault was a blockade of the Confederate shipyards at Norfolk, Virginia, to ensure that no Rebel warships could get in or out to support the operation. So in January 1862, a huge force of Union frigates parked themselves in the entrance to the Chesapeake Bay, essentially building a disagreeable wall of wood, sails, and cannons and daring the Rebels to do something about it.

But the South wasn't about to just lie down and let someone drop hundreds of thousands of enemy soldiers on her shores without at least putting up a decent fight. The Rebels had a plan to punch through the enemy blockade, reopen the waterways, and destroy the Northern invasion before it happened...and they had a secret weapon to help them make sure they succeeded.

A warship made out of iron. The first of its kind. The CSS *Virginia*.

When the US Navy abandoned the Norfolk Navy Yard at

the outbreak of the war, they'd burned most of their ships, but the Confederates took one of the frigates that was still in decent condition, the 263-foot USS *Merrimack*, and upgraded her like an iPhone, encasing the entire ship in four inches of sloped iron plating, loading her up with ten cannons, adding a couple of steam engines, and sticking a fearsome-looking four-foot-long iron ram on the end of her to rip gnarly holes in enemy ships and send them plummeting to the bottom of the ocean. When they were done, the Rebels were so excited they renamed it the *Virginia*. The Union still called it the *Merrimack*, though, because that was their name for it and they liked that much better than *Virginia*, anyway.

Construction on the *Virginia* was completed on March 5, 1862. Her maiden voyage would change the history of naval warfare forever—and mess up a lot of warships in the process.

When the *Virginia* set out on March 8, most of her crew were under the impression that this was going to be a training mission—you know, something to make sure that a ship made out of iron could actually float without taking on water and sinking. But Captain Franklin Buchanan had other plans entirely. He was going to see exactly what this baby was capable of. He fearlessly sailed right into the entire enemy blockading fleet.

Encased in thirty-five-degree sloped iron-and-steel plating, the *Virginia* was utterly undeterred by anything the Union navy had to throw at it. Belching black smoke and hurling ferocious steel-and-iron cannonballs from ten gun ports along her hull, the *Virginia* audaciously lurched ahead in a white-knuckled charge at the USS *Cumberland*—a towering, fifty-gun Union warship that had dominated the high seas for the last twenty years.

As you can probably imagine, the five Union warships of the blockading fleet didn't waste much time before turning every single one of their guns in the direction of the hideous metal monstrosity. Unfortunately for them, all they could do was watch in horror as even their biggest and most powerful cannon rounds bounced harmlessly off the iron hull like basketballs. The *Virginia* blitzed ahead, unfazed by the chaos, her iron ram pointed directly at the hull of the *Cumberland*. On her way to the Union flagship, she unleashed a sail-by broadside, blasting the fifty-gun USS *Congress* so intensely that it caught fire and ran aground. Then, as the rest of the blockading fleet watched, the *Virginia* crippled the *Cumberland* with a vicious broadside of cannon fire, then drove the tip of her ram into the *Cumberland*'s belly, shredding the wooden ship into flotsam and hitting her so hard it snapped off the ram and left a chunk of metal inside the Union vessel (which sounds rather uncomfortable, if you ask me). The *Cumberland* valiantly fired back at the *Virginia*, but her fifty cannons failed to make so much as a dent in the armor of the iron Confederate leviathan. The *Cumberland* sank in minutes, taking 121 crew members with her.

With the *Cumberland* down, the *Virginia* turned her attention to the *Congress*, which had run aground earlier in the fight and was now helplessly stuck on a sandbar. The *Virginia* sailed up beside her, loaded her guns with "hot shot"—cannonballs that were heated in a special furnace until they were so hot that they glowed red—and unleashed a brutal volley that set the wooden frigate *Congress* on fire in several places. The fire spread to the ammunition stores, blowing the ship into smithereens and killing over 120 crew members. One guy on the *Congress* did get a lucky shot with his rifle and hit the *Virginia*'s captain in the groin with a musket ball, but it was only a small consolation.

The *Virginia* spent the rest of the day playing Whac-A-Mole with the Union navy, but a busted smokestack limited her effectiveness somewhat. She ran the other three Union warships—the frigates *Minnesota*, *Roanoke*, and *St. Lawrence*—aground, but the tides forced the *Virginia* to withdraw to deeper waters before she could finish them off. By the end of the day, the *Virginia* had sunk two warships, grounded three more, and inflicted over four hundred casualties. It would be the worst destruction the US Navy would experience until the Japanese bombing of Pearl Harbor in World War II.

The next morning, March 9, 1862, the *Virginia* set out to finish the job she'd started the day before. The Union ships were still stuck aground, and it was obvious that old-school wooden frigates were no match for a fully armed-and-operational ironclad warship in a straight-up slugfest. To the crew of the CSS *Virginia*, all that remained was to put the Union blockade out of its misery once and for all.

When they reached the mouth of the Chesapeake Bay, however, the crew of the *Virginia* noticed that an unwelcome guest had joined the party—the USS *Monitor*. She was the North's secret weapon, a 172-foot-long Union gunboat that boasted four-inch-thick iron plating and featured two eleven-inch cannons mounted on a heavily armored revolving iron turret.

The stage was set for the first-ever battle between metal warships.

The *Monitor*, her crew angry about the carnage wrought by the *Virginia* and eager to take advantage of the element of surprise, steamed toward her enemy like a bat out of Hades. The *Virginia* loaded her cannons, turned them toward the oncoming ship, and waited for the *Monitor* to get in range for a volley.

The first barrage was fired around nine AM, as the *Virginia* unleashed a broadside at the oncoming *Monitor*. The *Monitor*, unfazed by the dozens of deadly cannonballs hurling toward her at incredibly high speeds, bravely steamed ahead in a single-minded mission to prove to this Rebel warship that the *Virginia* wasn't the scariest thing on the high seas. The *Monitor* closed to fighting distance, loaded her weapons as Confederate shells bounced off her heavy

plate armor, and unleashed a pair of gigantic shots from the twin cannons mounted in her turret.

What followed was basically the naval version of two knights in shining armor whaling on each other with swords and axes as hard as they possibly could, smashing each other in a frantic attempt to penetrate the other's defenses and deal a crippling wound. From less than a hundred yards away—shorter than the length of a single football field—these iron behemoths blasted each other with everything they had, their obscenely big cannons pounding huge dents in the opposing vessel's armor and ripping off her smokestacks. The *Virginia* tried to ram the *Monitor* with her hastily rebuilt battering ram, but the hateful iron lance clanged harmlessly off the sloped iron armor of the Union ship. The *Monitor* returned fire, but another glancing blow bounced harmlessly off the *Virginia*'s hull armor.

After nearly four hours of nonstop battle, the crew of the *Virginia* changed up their tactics—instead of trying to destroy the turret and guns of the *Monitor*, they started to aim at the less armored pilothouse, the spot where the ship's captain and pilot were stationed. An explosive shell scored a direct hit, sending shrapnel into the face of *Monitor* captain John L. Worden, temporarily blinding him with a white-hot chunk of superheated metal. With her captain injured and her ammunition low, the *Monitor* pulled back. The *Virginia*, taking on water in several places, was happy for the break and withdrew back to Norfolk.

In the end, even though the CSS *Virginia* slapped around quite a few ships and (temporarily) put out the *Monitor* captain's eyes, it wasn't enough to break the Union blockade of the Chesapeake Bay. The *Virginia* returned to port and never engaged the Union blockade fleet again. The Union forces landed at Yorktown, captured it, then marched across land and captured Norfolk on May 9 without ever actually having to fight the *Virginia* again. Rather than let the Union have their beloved ship, the crew of the *Virginia* pulled all the cannons off her and sank the ship before they left town, then headed north to join the defense of Richmond. Their courageous attack would be the closest the Confederacy would come to breaking the Union naval blockade.

Even though the battle was pretty indecisive (it was called a strategic Union victory), the message was heard loud and clear by all the navies of the world: Wood boats just weren't going to cut it anymore. After hearing the tales of the *Virginia* wrecking Union wooden ships like they were nothing, the navies of France, England, and half a dozen other European countries (not to mention the US and Confederate navies) started replacing their out-of-date wood boats with top-of-the-line iron-armored vessels.

And that, folks, is why you don't see wooden navy boats anymore.

The Anaconda Plan

The Union naval blockade was part of the US strategy known as
the Anaconda Plan. Completely unrelated to the Ice Cube/Jennifer
Lopez movie, the Anaconda Plan was designed by General Winfield
Scott as a method for squeezing the Confederates into submission
like a constrictor snake by cutting off their contact with the outside
world. It called for two things—a naval blockade of the Atlantic
and the Gulf to prevent the Rebels from importing weapons and
supplies from Europe, and the capture of the Mississippi River and
its major tributaries to split the Confederacy in half. Once these
two things were in place, the Union would then be able to clamp
down and force the South to depend on its own internal resources.
With no factories, industry, or weapon-making capabilities to speak
of, the Confederacy would be unable to continue fighting the war.

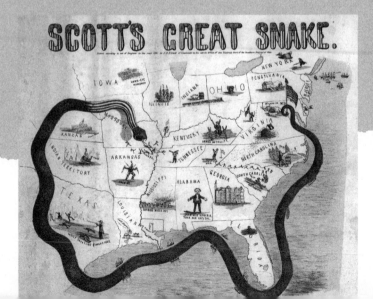

The First Ironclad

The first use of ironclad warships in battle was in 1592, when ultra-tough Korean admiral Yi Sun-sin developed something called "turtle ships," which sound kind of lame but were actually totally awesome, fast-moving warships with reinforced metal plating completely covering the top deck to protect the sailors from enemy arrows and gunfire. These metal plates had big steel spikes sticking out of them to discourage boarding parties, and each turtle ship carried about thirty guns. As an excellent addition, the front of it was shaped like a cool-looking dragon that shot a flamethrower out of its mouth, had a smokescreen that came out of its nose, and could be used as a battering ram to crunch enemy ships into driftwood. Yi used these early-model ironclads to barrel straight through the enemy lines, pinball around their formation BrickBreaker-style, ram the enemy flagship, then set the enemy commander on fire with a dragon-headed blowtorch before he could coordinate a counterattack and/or figure out how he was supposed to stop this gigantic steel-plated nautical bowling ball.

The Mason-Dixon Line

Named after the two guys who drew it, Charles Mason and Jeremiah Dixon, the Mason-Dixon Line was the result of an epic border dispute between Maryland and Pennsylvania that got so intense it required a special tag team of master surveyors to be brought in from England to deal with it. The 325-mile line, drawn between 1763 and 1767, is nowadays mostly remembered as serving as the official dividing line between free and slave states.

The Battle of Hampton Roads

Sailors

Union: 1,400

Confederate: 188

Casualties

Union: 369

Confederate: 24

Result

Union Victory

Ship Comparison

Ship Name:	CSS *Virginia*	USS *Monitor*
Displacement:	4,100 tons	1,003 tons
Length:	263 feet	172 feet
Speed:	4 knots	6 knots
Crew:	320 officers and crew	47 crew, 10 officers
Armament:	Two 7-inch rifled cannons	Two 11-inch smoothbore cannons
	Two 6.4-inch rifled cannons	
	Six 9-inch smoothbore cannons	
	Two 12-inch howitzers	

USS *Monitor*

CSS *Virginia*

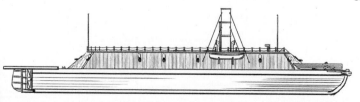

Shiloh

The Battle of Shiloh

Pittsburg Landing, Tennessee * April 6–7, 1862

> I saw an open field in our possession the second day, over which the Confederates had made repeated charges the day before, so covered with dead that it would have been possible to walk across the clearing, in any direction, stepping on dead bodies, and without a foot touching the ground.
>
> —General Ulysses S. Grant, US Army

THE BATTLE OF SHILOH IS THE HEART-stopping tale of the overall commander of all Confederate forces and the most popular and highly regarded commander the South possessed at the beginning of the war. The only ranking US Army general to join the Confederacy. A man who was initially offered the chance to lead Union forces, but went with his heart, declined, and sided with his native South.

That's right: I'm talking about...Albert Sidney Johnston. Yes, *the* Albert Sidney Johnston.

What, you've never heard of him?

Albert Sidney Johnston had a long, storied career busting heads from coast to coast across North America. He'd stared down his saber blade at tomahawk-wielding American Indian warrior braves during the Black Hawk War. When his adopted home of Texas decided to break away from Mexico in the 1830s, Johnston enlisted in the Texas Army as a private—the lowest rank possible—and within a year he was the most senior brigadier general in the army, fighting with Sam Houston and Jim Bowie against the armies of General Antonio López de Santa Anna. When the Mexican-American War went down, he left Texas, rejoined the US Army, served under future president Zachary Taylor, and saved the day during the Battle of Monterrey. When he was done with that, he became the first commander of the Second US Cavalry, led an expedition to battle Mormon separatists in Utah in 1857, and eventually found himself in command of all US forces on the West Coast by 1860. When the Civil War broke out, President Lincoln personally offered to make Johnston second-in-command of the entire United States military. He declined and told Lincoln he was going to join the South to be with his Texas brethren instead. Lincoln sent troops to capture him and prevent this from happening, but Johnston escaped, joined a unit known as the Los Angeles Mounted Rifles, rode from California to Texas on horseback, and immediately assumed overall command of all Confederate military forces west of the Appalachian Mountains.

So, yeah. He was kind of a big deal.

When he took command, Johnston had his work cut out for him. He was badly outnumbered, undersupplied, and forced to defend a three-hundred-mile-wide battlefront with just forty-five thousand barefoot men armed with what basically amounted to their grandpa's old varmint-hunting rifles and the shotgun they used to keep under the bed just in case a

bear tried to break into their house. Even worse, the man opposing him was probably the single toughest skull-busting maniac the North had to offer—Ulysses S. Grant, a thirty-nine-year-old, hard-as-nails Ohioan whose primary goal in life was squishing Rebels under his boots.

Grant's plan was simple—he was going to take 125,000 well-armed, well-trained, highly equipped men, support them with an armada of state-of-the-art gunboats, and ram them down the throat of the Confederacy with extreme prejudice until all that remained of the Rebellion was a pile of dead traitorous corpses.

Grant's primary objective was to capture the Mississippi River and its tributaries. By securing the largest river in the United States, trashing every bridge across it, and obliterating every Rebel fort he could find, Grant would not only cut the Confederacy in half but also have the perfect highway to transport troops, supplies, ammunition, and other dangerous things deep into the heart of enemy territory.

Albert Sidney Johnston did his best, fighting delaying actions, bluffing where he could, and trying to stop this ferocious blue-jacketed onslaught, but things got out of hand in a hurry. Grant pressed the attack whenever possible...even when he had direct orders from his superiors not to. In the early days of the war out west, he captured two major forts, secured a couple of major rivers, conquered Kentucky and most of Tennessee, occupied Nashville, and was such an uncompromising warrior that the Union newspapers joked that the "U. S." in his name stood for "Unconditional Surrender."

If Johnston was going to have any chance of turning the tide of this war, he was going to need to do something drastic. And he was going to have to do it soon.

In early April 1862, he found as good an opportunity as any. Grant had just crossed the Tennessee River, docked his transports at a place called Pittsburg Landing, and unloaded about forty-three thousand troops onto the other side. His plan was to wait for Union general Don Carlos Buell to show up with another twenty-three thousand men, join forces, and together march into Mississippi and start tearing things apart.

Albert Sidney Johnston's plan was bold, but given that his only other option was "Hey, let's sit back while they form a mega-army and trample me into dust," it was as good a chance as he was going to get. First, he'd mass almost his entire army—forty-five thousand men—stack them up in one formidable ancient Greek–style phalanx, sneak them through the forest, and launch a bayonet-thrusting surprise attack that would try to knock Grant's army out of commission with one Mike Tyson haymaker sucker punch. If Johnston could capture Pittsburg Landing quickly with one massive assault, he might have time to reorganize his men and defend the crossing against Buell's army. Success would give the Confederates the victory they needed to change the tide of the war in the west. Defeat would be crushing. It was time to roll the dice.

On the morning of April 6, 1862, Johnston assembled his men, raised his sword, and vowed that this night they would water their horses in the Tennessee River. The biggest battle America had yet seen was about to begin.

Grant's forces (who had basically spent the last several

months busting grills everywhere they could find them) really didn't expect any crazy stuff to go down on this particular morning, so instead of digging trenches and building defensive positions, they just camped out in the open, talked about girls, played cards, and waited for Buell's troops to show up. So when they were rudely awoken at five o'clock in the morning by the sounds of men screaming and peeked outside their tent flaps to see forty thousand shrieking Confederate soldiers sprinting toward them out of the woods, firing shotguns and muskets all over the place and waving bayonet-equipped rifles around like they meant it, they were more than a little surprised.

With a mighty charge, the Confederates burst from the trees and swarmed through the Union camps, kicking over tents and carts, setting fire to wagons, trading in their beat-up old family hunting rifles for state-of-the-art modern rifled muskets the Union troops left behind, and generally just causing all sorts of destruction. Union soldiers, some still in their underwear, grabbed their rifles and tried to desperately fall back to defensive positions, fighting for their lives as the chaos of battle swirled around them in every direction. Many of the men on either side were seeing their first real live-fire combat, so instead of a disciplined battle, this engagement was more like a back-alley down-and-dirty fistfight between two rough-and-tumble bare-knuckled brawlers.

One of Grant's commanders, the soon-to-be-infamous General William Tecumseh Sherman, rallied his troops around the tiny Shiloh Church, a place that ironically took its name from the Hebrew word for "place of peace," but now gives its name to one of the most gruesome battlefields in American history. Sherman tried to hold his position, but Albert Sidney Johnston's ferocious legions devastated his lines, forcing Sherman to retreat to defensive positions at Pittsburg Landing.

With the Union lines crumbling around him in a typhoon of screaming Rebels, two Northern commanders—a Missouri rope-maker named Benjamin Prentiss and an Illinois lawyer named W. H. L. Wallace, who had risen from private to major general—received strict orders from Grant: Hold the line at all costs.

They dug in on an old trail, and with Johnston's Confederates furiously bearing down on them, the Union line prepared to withstand one of the most ruthless Confederate attacks of the war. If they fell here, nothing was standing between the Rebel horde and Pittsburg Landing—they absolutely had to hold the line if they wanted to give Grant's army any time to regroup.

For almost seven hours, the fate of the west hung in the balance. Prentiss's and Wallace's divisions poured fire into the enemy, filling the air with so many bullets that it sounded like a swarm of bees had shown up. Dubbed the "Hornet's Nest" for this reason by the Southerners, the defensive position quickly piled up with bodies of wounded and dying men as the Union soldiers, mostly farm boys from Iowa, Missouri, and Illinois, took the brunt of everything the Confederacy had to offer. Nearly a dozen attacks were made on their positions, the Rebels bravely and ferociously rushing into a torrent of gunfire, but all twelve times the North hurled the Confederates back with a hail of bullets. Despite having over sixty-two Confederate cannons pounding their position, and with the rest of the Union army crumbling to dust around them, the men of the Hornet's Nest clung to their posts by their fingernails.

Albert Sidney Johnston, realizing that his entire plan hinged on capturing this position, personally rode up to the front to inspire his men for one final, desperate attack. Drawing his sword, he spurred his horse ahead and shouted for his men to follow him to glory, and then the overall commander of Confederate forces in the west personally led the final, daring charge straight on at the enemy.

The Rebel army, inspired by this unbelievable act of bravery by their commander, renewed their charge once again. Johnston was nicked in the leg by a stray bullet, but the big, strong, strapping Confederate commander refused any medical attention. It was just a scratch, and he wasn't going to be slowed down by some stupid paper cut, especially at the moment of what was about to be the Confederacy's greatest victory.

Less than an hour later Albert Sidney Johnston turned pale, slumped off his horse, and fell to the turf. When his assistant took off Johnston's boot, it was filled with blood. The "grazing shot" had nicked a major artery in Johnston's leg—an easily treatable wound if he'd just taken the time to examine it—and he'd bled to death right there on the battle-field. He would be the highest-ranking military commander on either side to be killed in the battle, and his death would be a heartbreaking loss for the Confederacy.

Albert Sidney Johnston was succeeded by Pierre Gustave Toutant Beauregard, the Louisianan who had started the Civil War by ordering the attack on Fort Sumter. By five thirty PM, after an eternity of a day facing withering destruction at the hands of bitter Rebel troops, the 2,200 survivors of Benjamin Prentiss's shattered division, completely surrounded and tak-ing fire from all sides, finally surrendered to soldiers of the Nineteenth Tennessee Infantry.

Despite the urging of his brigade commanders, Beaure-gard didn't have the killer instinct of Johnston, and he ordered his men to call off the attack and make camp for the night. As far as Beauregard was concerned, he had the Yankees right where he wanted them, and he could destroy them in the morning, after he'd had a chance to resupply and regroup his own forces.

That night, under the cover of darkness, Major General Don Carlos Buell arrived with more than twenty thousand fresh Union soldiers. It took all night to ferry them across the Tennessee River.

When the Confederates awoke the next day, ready to pick up right where they left off and drive Grant's army back into the river, they had no idea they were now facing the combined might of two Federal armies.

The Rebels attacked. They hit a wall. Then the Union troops surged forward from their positions, eager for revenge.

Grant ordered a full assault, and waves of blue came pouring out of Pittsburg Landing. The Confederate attack stalled, then fell, and over the course of the day was slowly pushed farther and farther back. By nightfall the Rebels were in full retreat. Their gambit had failed.

Not only was the Battle of Shiloh the bloodiest battle in American history up until that point, but the 23,716 casualties—13,047 Union and 10,669 Confederate—was more men than had been killed or wounded in *every single previous war in American history combined*. It was becoming painfully obvious that this country had a fight on its hands, and that it was going to take more than one megacharge and a little bravado to end this war.

Sadly, it would only get worse.

Young Soldiers

The average age of a soldier in the Civil War was twenty-five, but some sources estimate that the Union army alone had over one hundred thousand boys under fifteen years old serving in its ranks. Younger kids, ages nine to twelve or so, were used as runners, drummer boys, naval ship cabin boys, and assistants on artillery crews, but it would be just as common to see them shouldering muskets and rushing into combat.

Rebel Yell

One of the most characteristic aspects of the Confederate army was the terrifying Rebel yell—a spine-chilling yee-haw-style screech described as "the ugliest sound that any mortal ever heard." According to one anonymous Federal soldier, "There is nothing like it on this side of the infernal region. The peculiar corkscrew sensation that it sends down your backbone under these circumstances can never be told. You have to feel it."

Extra, Extra, Read All About It

Thanks to the development of the telegraph, the Civil War was the first war where newspaper reporters showed up on the front lines and wrote live dispatches from the field. Roughly four hundred war correspondents and newsmen braved heavy fire and dangerous battlefields to bring firsthand accounts of the battle to anxious readers back home, who bought up papers by the thousands to catch a glimpse of what was happening in the war. Of course, as is still the case today, this wasn't always appreciated by the generals. When William Tecumseh Sherman received word that three reporters were blown up by Confederate artillery one morning, he responded by saying, "Good, now we shall have news from Hell before breakfast."

The Battle of Shiloh

Troops

Union: 65,085

Confederate: 44,968

Casualties

Union: 13,047

Confederate: 10,669

Result

Union Victory

Other Civil Wars

Civil war wasn't exactly a new concept in 1861, and the United States is far from being the only country in the world where former citizens of the same place actively tried to kill one another with reckless abandon. Here are some of the more well-known civil wars from around the world:

The Fall of the Roman Republic (134–44 BC)

With the Roman Senate getting all up in his business about how he shouldn't use his legendary popularity and overwhelming military superiority to seize control of the Republic, Roman general Gaius Julius Caesar, a hero of several wars against the Gauls, marched his legion across the Rubicon River, captured Rome, set himself up as dictator, and then destroyed the armies of anybody who had a problem with it. Not long afterward Caesar was stabbed to death by angry senators, but his adopted son, Octavian, took care of that when he had the rebellious senators killed, destroyed a couple more armies, dissolved the republic, and set himself up as the first emperor of Rome.

Three Kingdoms of China (AD 220–280)

With the death of the last emperor of the Han Dynasty in AD 220, the most powerful and longest-running empire China had ever seen quickly disintegrated into chaos. In the years that followed, three powerful kingdoms seized control of large chunks of the countryside—the warlord

Cao Cao dominated everything north of the Yangtze River, and the kingdoms of Shu and Wu ruled lands to the south. Naturally, all three tried to kill one another and rebuild the empire, and the resulting civil war lasted sixty years and left millions of people dead. Ultimately, Cao Cao's Wei Kingdom united the land under one banner, and as soon as that was done, Wei's chief military advisor killed the new king and seized power, installing the Jin Dynasty.

Warring States of Japan (1467–1600)

The height of the Japanese medieval period, the warring states was a century of near-constant warfare that rocked Japan. Even though there was technically a shogun and an emperor in charge of everything during this time period, neither of those dudes had a lot of power, and the only way Japan was going to figure out whose cuisine reigned supreme was for every samurai in the land to draw his katana and start slashing his enemies to pieces. It all culminated in the Battle of Sekigahara, the largest land battle ever fought on Japanese soil, where 160,000 samurai and foot soldiers battled it out for ultimate control of the country.

The English Civil War (1642–1649)

When the British Parliament decided they were tired of fighting stupid wars for King Charles I and refused to appropriate funds for them, the English king dissolved the Parliament and decided, forget it, I'm going to be the only guy in charge here. Both sides raised troops and, led by the infamous Oliver Cromwell and his brilliant New Model Army, Parliament forces defeated the loyalists after a series of intense battles across the English countryside. Charles I was executed by beheading, Cromwell seized power as Lord Protector of the Realm (basically another king), and after Cromwell died, everybody said, eh, whatever, and invited Charles's son, Charles II, to be king.

The Russian Revolution (1917–1922)

On November 7, 1917, Communist supporters of Vladimir Lenin stormed the palace of Tsar Nicholas II, killing the Russian emperor and his entire family and beginning a civil war that would spread across the country. Founded by Bolshevik leader Leon Trotsky, the Communist Red Army mobilized peasants and workers across Russia into battle against the aristocratic supporters of the tsar. Despite the loyalists receiving cash and troops from basically every Western country from the United States to Germany (all terrified of the prospect of a world power being run by a Communist government), the Red Army recruited over 1.5 million troops, overran Moscow, and turned imperial Russia into the Soviet Union.

The Spanish Civil War (1936–1939)

In 1936, pro-Nazi military commanders in Spain attempted to overthrow the democratically elected government, rising up in battle and attempting to install the army's leader, General Francisco Franco, as dictator for

life. Fascist-hating freedom-lovers from across the world
flocked to Spain to help fight the forces of Franco (including an American unit known as the Abraham Lincoln Brigade), but overwhelming military technology and aid from
Adolf Hitler's Nazi Germany was too much to overcome—
Franco took power by seizing Madrid at the head of a fully
operational mechanized and industrialized army on March
28, 1939. The Nazis would use the experience they gained
fighting this war to help them get off to a head start on
World War II.

The Cleopatra of the Secession

Belle Boyd's Wartime Exploits

1861–1864 ✳ Shenandoah Valley, Virginia

> A gold palmetto tree beneath her beautiful chin, a Rebel soldier's belt around her waist, and a velvet band across her forehead with the seven stars of the Confederacy shedding their pale light therefrom...the only additional ornament she required to render herself perfectly beautiful was a Yankee noose encircling her neck.
>
> —*New-York Tribune*

BELLE BOYD WAS A HARDCORE SOUTHERN woman who took the Union occupation of her hometown pretty personally and became one of the boldest and most daring spies of the Civil War. She undertook brazen midnight

rides through enemy territory, smuggling coded messages to
Stonewall Jackson in the middle of raging battlefields, and
generally resembled a mid-nineteenth-century cross between a
Scarlett O'Hara Southern belle and a backwoods country girl
hunting varmints on her grandpa's farm. During three years
as an unconquerable Rebel spy, Belle delivered thousands of
messages, was arrested six times, was imprisoned three times,
and was deported twice, yet none of this deterred her from her
mission to ensure the survival of the Confederate States of
America.

With most of the war being fought in the South, and many
towns in Northern Virginia and Tennessee passing back and
forth between Confederate liberators and Union occupiers, a
lot of Southern women ended up getting largely unwelcome
front-row seats to the battlefields of the Civil War. Southern
troops would build fortifications outside the town; the Federals
would storm the town, capture it, commandeer the townspeo-
ple's homes, turn them into troop quarters or hospitals, then
move on to the next place a few weeks later. Sometimes the
Rebels would come back, retake the town, and drive off the Yankees. If the townsfolk were lucky, their wood houses wouldn't
catch on fire and cannonballs wouldn't end up lodged in their
dining room tables in the process.

Maria Isabella Boyd was seventeen years old in 1861, the
oldest of eight kids in a prosperous family, when the Civil
War came to her hometown of Martinsburg, Virginia. Federal

troops took the town without a fight and occupied it, and then one night some drunken fool stumbled into the Boyds' home, ripped a Confederate flag down from their porch, and said some incredibly threatening and mean-spirited things to Maria and her mother. The Boyds demanded this knucklehead leave, but when he got a little too aggressive, Maria—better known as Belle—drew a pocket-sized pistol out from her petticoat and stone-cold capped him with a single round to the dome. The dude's commanding officer came by the next morning to see what the goat cheese had happened there, and when he heard the Boyds' version of events, he was so convinced of his man's impropriety that he didn't even press charges against Belle.

But the clemency and understanding the Federal officer showed Belle Boyd wasn't what she remembered about the incident. She was livid, and swore from that point on to do everything in her power to aid the Rebellion and get these Yankees out of her town.

Operating from the hotel her father owned in Front Royal, Virginia, Belle Boyd immediately began gathering information about what the Yankee army was up to. Working in a completely unofficial capacity, Belle started hanging around the hotel, going to parties at the Union camp, and sneaking around under the cover of darkness, either eavesdropping on Union officers or sweet-talking them with her charm. Then she'd take that info, ride through Federal lines to the Confederate camp, and relay it to the first officer she could find.

Before long, Rebel spymasters were hooking her up with ciphers and secret codes to transmit encrypted messages, and the infamous "Cleopatra of the Secession" was born.

Throughout 1861 and early 1862, Belle Boyd brought coded messages to James Earl Brown ("Jeb") Stuart and Stonewall Jackson, not only providing them with much-needed info on where the Union forces were stationed and how many guys they had, but also stealing gunpowder, morphine, and bullets from Federal camps and sneaking them out inside her gigantic hoop skirt. She also managed to engineer a profitable racket on the side when Confederate privates could pay her a couple of bucks to smuggle letters or booze in or out of Federal lines. This worked out pretty well for the most part, except for one time when a Southern soldier refused to pay—she slugged him in the jaw, and the ensuing benches-clearing camp brawl left thirty Rebel soldiers injured.

Flirtatious, direct, stealthy, and fearless, Belle Boyd defied all social conventions about what a Southern lady should be, but as long as she got the job done she didn't care.

La Belle Rebelle's shining moment in the war came during the Shenandoah Valley Campaign in 1862. With Union armies marching south from DC and up from the peninsula, already-legendary Confederate general Stonewall Jackson was sent to Belle's hood with orders to somehow slow down an army of sixty thousand Union troops and prevent them from linking up with the other two armies. Jackson, with just seventeen thousand

guys, needed all the help he could get. Even if Belle's dad weren't serving as an infantryman under Jackson, she would have done everything she could to ensure the success of his mission.

For nearly thirty days, Boyd went on midnight rides through enemy territory, stealing or soliciting military secrets from Union troops and relaying them to Jackson, occasionally running through gunfire from Federal pickets in the process. One time she asked two handsome Union cavalrymen to escort her home, led them to Confederate lines, and handed them over as prisoners of war. Another time she rode her horse straight onto the battlefield during the Battle of Front Royal, charging through cannon fire in a white petticoat, waving her bonnet around her head as Federal musket fire kicked up dirt around her horse's hooves. She had bullet holes in her clothing as she approached Jackson's top aide, telling him that the Union center was incredibly weak because it was maneuvering for a trap. Jackson charged ahead and steamrolled the Federal center before they could spring it, winning the day with a tremendous victory.

Jackson's campaign ended up being a lights-out success, with the famous Confederate general marching his men 245 miles in thirty-five days, winning five battles, and knocking the Union troops out of action just in time to race back and help Robert E. Lee defend Richmond from George McClellan's forces. La Belle Rebelle, the so-called Southern Joan of Arc, was made an honorary captain and aide-de-camp to Stonewall

Jackson, and he allowed her to attend a troop review before he headed out of the Shenandoah Valley for Richmond.

During the campaign Belle Boyd had been detained about a half-dozen times, but thanks to her ability to talk her way out of most situations, she'd done only one week of prison time total in the early years of the war. This changed in June 1862, when it turned out her new boyfriend was actually a Union spy pretending to be a Rebel soldier, and she was arrested, brought to Washington, DC, and put into the Old Capitol Prison. Not even hardcore jail time stopped the Cleopatra of the Secession from doing her thing, however—she hung smuggled Confederate flags through the bars of her cell, sang "Dixie" all day long, and had a setup where she would eavesdrop on guards and prisoners for extra info. At night a Confederate spy would shoot rubber balls into her cell with a bow and arrow and she'd sew messages into them and throw them back.

After four weeks in the pen, Boyd was freed in a prisoner exchange, but a few months later she found herself back in prison. This time she was deported to Quebec, but Belle Boyd, the petticoated female James Bond, somehow hooked up with Rebel agents in Canada, received a few dispatches from Jefferson Davis to the British prime minister, and headed to England on a steamer ship to hand-deliver them. On the way out she was detained by Federal officers, but amazingly she convinced them she was headed to England to get treatment for typhus or some other weird illness. They searched her, found nothing, and let her go.

Boyd tried to hitch a ride back to the South aboard a Confederate blockade runner in 1864, but her ship was overrun by a Union ship and captured and she was detained as a prisoner of war. Incredibly, Belle Boyd fell in love with the Federal ship's commander, Lieutenant Sam Hardinge, and persuaded him not only to let her go but to go AWOL from his post, abandon the navy, elope to Canada, get married, and move to England.

After the war Boyd wrote a memoir, which, as you might imagine, became an instant bestseller, both in the North and the South. After Hardinge eventually died, she married a British actor half her age and spent the rest of her life on tour, giving public readings of her story. She died in 1900 at the age of fifty-seven, while on tour in Wisconsin.

Spy-Speak

Since most messages between secret agents were conveyed using a telegraph—a mode of communication that could easily be tapped by someone who knew what they were doing—Union and Confederate agents had to devise elaborate systems, decoder rings, and other ways of masking their transmissions so that any spy-hunters who were listening in would just hear a bunch of gibbering madness that apparently made no sense whatsoever.

The Shenandoah Valley Campaign

Troops
Union: 60,000

Confederate: 17,000

Casualties
Union: 4,500

Confederate: 2,500

Result
Confederate Victory

Women in the War

One Confederate officer who fought boldly in the war's early years was Lieutenant Harry Buford, an Arkansas man who raised his own battalion of troops, was on the front lines at the Battle of Bull Run, was wounded at Fort Donelson, and then was wounded a second time by a stray artillery shell while burying the dead following the fighting on the first day at Shiloh. When Buford was taken to the doctor for his wound, the doctor cut away his uniform and was very surprised to find that Lieutenant Buford was, in fact, a twenty-year-old Cuban-American woman named Loreta Janeta Velazquez. Velazquez was discharged from the army and spent the rest of the war as a double agent operating deep behind enemy lines.

Velazquez's story, as told through her unbelievably over-the-top autobiography, has been picked apart by historians over the years, but there is no doubt that some of the toughest women on either side of the Mason-Dixon Line dressed up in full battle gear, disguised themselves as men, and fought on the front lines for what they believed in. In his memoirs, one private from the Eleventh Illinois, fighting outside Dallas in 1864, even mentioned a company that featured several female troops assaulting his regiment's line. He told his father in a letter that "they fought like demons." The general consensus among historians is that there were probably three hundred to five hundred female soldiers in the Civil War. Here are a few:

Nancy Hart Douglas

When Union troops killed her brother-in-law, North Carolina–born Nancy Hart joined a pro-Confederate guerilla cavalry unit operating out of West Virginia. Using her knowledge of the Southern terrain and her excellent horsemanship and rifle skills, Hart worked as a scout, spy, and guerilla fighter, gathering info any way she could to help the cause. A reward was placed on her head, and she was eventually captured and imprisoned, but she seduced a Union trooper into handing over his pistol, killed him with it, jumped out a second-story window, stole a lieutenant colonel's horse, and rode for Rebel lines.

Kady Brownell

Born to a military family from Scotland, nineteen-year-old Kady Brownell and her newlywed husband enlisted in the First Rhode Island and went to war for the Union when the Civil War broke out. Kady, who never attempted to conceal her gender, was given the nickname "Daughter of the Regiment" and was trained in rifle marksmanship and sword fighting. She carried the regimental flag for both the First and Fifth Rhode Island, fought in several battles openly as a woman, and survived the war along with her husband. Her one stint at nursing didn't work out well, however—she helped out a wounded Confederate soldier, but when he opened his eyes he insulted her for being a woman soldier, and Sergeant Brownell drew her bayonet and ended him.

Jennie Hodgers

Born near Belfast, Ireland, Jennie Hodgers immigrated to the United States as a teenager by stowing away on a freight ship. In August 1862, at age eighteen, she enlisted in the Ninety-Fifth Illinois Infantry as "Albert D. J. Cashier," and served throughout the war without ever being discovered as a woman. Fighting with Grant's Army of the Tennessee, Hodgers battled as a front-line infantry soldier in engagements from Vicksburg to Atlanta, charging head-on into enemy lines and surviving through the war without sustaining a single wound, even though over 280 of the men from her company died in battle. After the war she went home, continued to live as a man, and wasn't outed as a woman until she was on her deathbed in 1913.

Sarah Edmonds

Enlisting in the Second Michigan Infantry on her second attempt, Sarah Edmonds masqueraded as a male nurse in several of the early battles of the war. As she followed the Army of the Potomac through the Seven Days and Antietam, Sarah's talent for disguise came into play on an even greater scale late in 1862 when she was sent behind Confederate lines multiple times on deep-cover spy missions to gather intel on the enemy. Edmonds finished the war, received a pension, and was admitted to the Union army veterans' association, the Grand Army of the Republic.

Charlotte Hope

When her Confederate army fiancé was killed during a Union raid, Charlotte Hope disguised herself as "Charlie Hopper" and enlisted in Jeb Stuart's First Virginia Cavalry with a single plan—kill twenty-one Yankees, one for each year of her late fiancé's life. Refusing to be paid for her services, Hope volunteered for dangerous scouting missions and raids, and was a hard-fighting Rebel who engaged the enemy any time she encountered him. She was killed during a raid in Northern Virginia without mentioning whether or not she'd achieved her goal.

The Great Locomotive Chase

John Alfred Wilson's Wild Ride

April 12–November 10, 1862

> Experience has taught me that man, in the fix we were, is the worst and most desperate creature on earth, and will do things that seem utter impossibilities before their accomplishment.
>
> —Private John Alfred Wilson, Twenty-First Ohio Infantry

THE GREAT LOCOMOTIVE CHASE IS THE incredible tale of two Union troopers who went on a daring, almost suicidal sabotage mission deep behind enemy lines, got involved in a high-speed train chase spanning several counties, did battle with an entire regiment of Confederate troops, spent weeks on the run being pursued by virtually every able-bodied man in the Confederacy, and then became the first men to ever receive the Congressional Medal of Honor.

In April 1862, one of the Federal commanders, General Ormsby Mitchel, was looking to pull out all the stops in his single-minded effort to capture Chattanooga, Tennessee, and strike a decisive blow against a powerful Rebel stronghold. Unfortunately, since Chattanooga was just a short train ride away from a few hundred thousand Confederates in Atlanta, any attempt to capture the city was going to fail miserably unless the Union could cut the city off from reinforcements. If Mitchel was going to take Chattanooga, he was going to need an insane plan—and some insane men to execute it.

John Alfred Wilson was a twenty-nine-year-old private in the Twenty-First Ohio Infantry Regiment when the call came down that Federal high command was looking for two dozen deep-cover agents to volunteer for a suicide mission deep behind Confederate lines. Wilson, who was always looking to do awesome things, immediately signed up. He was paired with another man from his regiment, Private Mark Wood, and together these gutsy soon-to-be-saboteurs put on civilian clothes, crossed the border into Tennessee, and spent four days traveling by foot through enemy-controlled territory until they reached the railroad town of Marietta, Georgia. There, they linked up with eighteen other Union spies and espionage experts set on initiating one of the craziest raids in the entire war—they were going to gank a Confederate railroad car and scorched-earth vaporize the Rebel rail system all the way to Chattanooga.

Andrews' Raiders (so called because they were led by a man named Andrews) stuffed revolvers under their coats, boarded a train known as the *General* at Marietta Station, and, for the glory of the Union, these undercover Federal agents began riding it north toward Chattanooga. When everybody got off the train to get breakfast outside Kennesaw, Tennessee, Private Wilson and the rest of the raiders stormed the locomotive engine, commandeered the train, and peeled out of there like joyriding teenagers, leaving all the conductors and passengers in the dust wondering what just happened. These guys then immediately sped north, destroying the tracks behind them, cutting telegraph lines by swinging on them like Tarzan (no kidding), and torching a bunch of bridges in an effort to destroy the train link between Atlanta and Chattanooga.

This ridiculously dangerous attempt at sabotage would have worked, too, if it weren't for a completely irate Georgian named William Allen Fuller. Fuller was a conductor on the *General*, and when he saw that he was getting trainjacked by a bunch of Yankees, this mustachioed madman crammed a half ton of bacon in his mouth, kicked over his breakfast table, ran out of the restaurant, and started hauling after his runaway train on foot. Over the next fifty-one hours, Fuller pursued the *General* first on foot, then using one of those wacky hand-car things from the cartoons, and then by commandeering a southbound train, loading it up with stragglers from the First Georgia Infantry, throwing the locomotive in reverse, and pursuing the *General* while riding backward down the track. When Wilson and the raiders saw Fuller burning rubber toward them in reverse, they set a train car on fire and released the coupling so that it careened right at him, but Fuller just busted right through the wreckage and kept on rolling. With Fuller and the mad Georgians hot on their trail, the raiders ran out of steam, and the *General*, now completely out of fuel, slowly came to a halt along the tracks. Wilson and Wood jumped off the moving train and sprinted into the woods while musket balls whizzed past their heads.

But the locomotive chase was just the beginning of these Union spies' adventure. For the next thirty-six hours, Wilson and Wood were pursued through the mountains and forests of Tennessee by soldiers, civilians, and tracking dogs. After eluding capture during the night and talking their way out of what Wilson refers to as a "ticklish situation" (his term for being apprehended by a Confederate cavalry company and having the commander tell him, "We don't take prisoners—we execute them"), the fleeing men captured a boat, took it fifty miles down the Tennessee River, and nearly made it to Union lines. After bluffing a group of Confederate stragglers into thinking Wilson was just some inquisitive Georgia civilian,

the on-the-run Yankee spies learned that the Union army had just taken the town of Stevenson, Alabama, which was only a few miles from their location. Wilson and Wood walked to Stevenson, eager for their arduous ordeal to be over.

When they got there, they found it had already been retaken by the Rebels. Whoops.

Both Wilson and Wood were captured on sight, just seven miles from friendly lines. They were brought before the Confederate commander in the sector, a General Ledbetter, who took great pleasure in telling the men they were going to be hanged to death as spies and then thrown in an unmarked grave. Wilson handled the notification of his imminent death like a hero in an old cowboy movie: He looked Ledbetter in the eye and told him, "Hang me and be damned; but I tell you one thing to remember. If you ever do come across one of [our] men, and hang him, look out that sooner or later your own neck don't pay the penalty—because this hanging business will be quite common about the time this Rebellion closes up."

Ledbetter didn't take this very well.

Wilson and Wood were taken to Chattanooga, dragged through the streets in chains, and thrown into a horrible place affectionately known among the prisoners as "the Hole." It was there that Wilson learned he'd been the last of the raiders to be captured—the rest of the men were already down in the Hole waiting for him. Together, these twenty-two prisoners (the twenty train raiders, plus two other spies who were captured on their way to Marietta) spent the next five months in a thirteen-by-thirteen-foot unventilated, unlit dirt room in the basement of an old prison, baking away in the suffocating, airless heat of the stifling Tennessee summer. Their chains were never removed, their clothes became infested with lice, and their food consisted of cornmeal and rancid meat. Then, when Wilson and the men figured their lives couldn't possibly be any worse, the Confederates went out and hanged eight of the raiders for being spies (which they pretty much were).

After five months in the Hole, Wilson was transferred to much better conditions at Fulton County Prison in Atlanta, but he and the other thirteen remaining prisoners knew they had to get the heck out of there quickly if they wanted to continue being not dead. So one night, when the guard came to drop off their food, the raiders struck—they attacked the jailer, took his keys, opened all the cells, and attempted a breakout from a prison located right in the middle of Confederate-controlled Atlanta. Wilson fought his way out of there, first swinging around a loose brick he'd pried from the wall of his cell, and then throwing down with the guards barroom brawl–style and busting skulls with an empty bottle of whiskey he'd found in the barracks.

With the guards subdued by extreme bottle-swinging violence, John Wilson and the rest of the raiders rushed out of the jail, blitzed through the town, and jumped the city walls while musket balls cracked all around them. One shot hit so

close to the wooden wall that splinters from it shot up and
got into Wilson's leg, but he kept on trucking. The escapees
ran to the nearby woods, split up into groups of two, and ran
off in different directions to increase their chances of escape.

Wilson once again teamed up with his old friend Mark
Wood, and together they spent the next three days picking
their way through the woods while dogs and guys with guns
chased after them. They made it to the Chattahoochee River,
and then, realizing that everyone was expecting them to go
north, they made yet another in a long series of bold deci-
sions—they stole a boat and headed south toward Florida.
The two men crossed nearly three hundred miles in the next
thirty days, sailing downstream on a stolen boat, living off
the land, scavenging farmland at night for food, and fighting
alligators in the Florida swamps by hitting them with pad-
dles. They also hit a dolphin with a paddle because they didn't
know what it was, which is kind of funny if you think about
it. Half-dead, starving, sunburned, and suffering from mos-
quito bites, scurvy, and yellow fever, the men finally reached
the mouth of the Chattahoochee. In the distance, they saw
the ships of the Federal blockade, so they took a homemade
canoe out on the open water (they had to build their own
after their stolen boat was stolen back from them while they
were camped on shore one night), survived the high seas, and
got picked up by a Federal gunboat on November 10, 1862.
They were two of only eight escapees to make it home—the

rest were recaptured before crossing back to Union lines.

After sailing to Jamaica and a couple of other cool places with the gunboat, Wilson was brought back to Washington, DC, where he was promptly imprisoned for violating a mandatory curfew. Wilson got out of jail the next morning, met Abraham Lincoln, and was personally presented with the first-ever batch of Medals of Honor for his service to the US Army by the president himself. (Note: His award was presented in September 1863, rather than on March 25, 1863, with the rest of the raiders', but it's pretty much the same thing.) He would later rejoin his old unit, get married, write his memoirs, fight through the war, and live to be seventy-two, though not all in that order.

★ ★ ★

POW

Being a prisoner of war in the Civil War didn't mean that you were by any means safe. Since nobody expected the war to go on as long as it did, neither side built adequate prison facilities, and as a result most prisons were giant overcrowded messes that lacked important stuff like bathrooms, food, and medical care. Including the two most notorious prisons of the war—Andersonville in the South, where the situation was so bad the warden ended up being hanged for war crimes, and Elmyra in the North, where prisoners had to camp outside in the snow in the middle of the New York winter—roughly 12 to 15 percent of all Civil War POWs ended up dying in captivity.

The Great Locomotive Chase

Troops

Union: 20

Confederate: ~3,000

Casualties

Union: 20 captured, 8 executed

Confederate: ~10

Result

Confederate Victory

Unit Organization in the Civil War

Corps	2+ divisions	~20,000+ men	Major General
Division	3–4 brigades	~12,000 men	Major General
Brigade	4–6 regiments	~4000 men	Brigadier General
Regiment	10 companies	~1000 men	Colonel
Battalion	4–6 companies	~500 men	Major or Lieutenant Colonel
Company	—	~100 men	Captain

Note that these numbers were perfect-condition "on paper" strengths, not including sickness, death, and wounded men. In a battle situation, the average sizes of these units were far smaller—on average, about forty to fifty to a company, five hundred to a regiment, and one thousand to fifteen hundred to a brigade.

ARTILLERY

Artillery was organized differently:

Artillery Battalion: 3–5 batteries, 12–30 guns, 150–400 artillerymen, commanded by a lieutenant colonel or major

Artillery Battery: 4–6 guns, usually of the same caliber, organized into sections of two, with each section commanded by a lieutenant. 40–100 men, plus horses and ammo carts, etc. Batteries were commanded by a captain.

MILITARY RANKS

Enlisted Men: Private, Corporal, Sergeant, First Sergeant, Sergeant-Major

Junior Officers: Second Lieutenant, First Lieutenant, Captain, Major, Lieutenant Colonel, Colonel

General Officers: Brigadier General, Major General, Lieutenant General, General

Robert E. Lee in Northern Virginia

The Peninsula and Second Bull Run

Northern Virginia ∗ June 1–August 30, 1862

> It was not war—it was murder.
>
> —General D. H. Hill, Confederate army

ON MAY 31, 1862, OVERALL CONFEDERATE commander Joseph E. Johnston led his army into the rain-soaked, knee-deep mud outside the Fair Oaks train depot in a final attempt to keep the surging Union army from surrounding Richmond, laying siege to the city, and ending the war with one humiliating Confederate defeat. Johnston, seeing what he thought was a weakness in the Federal positions, issued a bunch of confusing orders handwritten on scraps of paper and ordered his units to march into a thick forest, where they immediately got lost, ran into one another, attacked the wrong place, and then got ingloriously mowed down by Union artillery. When Johnston rode up to the front lines to try to see what the heck was going on, he was shot in the shoulder by a sniper, got hit in the chest with artillery shrapnel, and fell off his horse, breaking his shoulder blade and a couple of ribs and knocking himself unconscious in the process.

It was not the Confederacy's finest hour.

The situation following the disaster at Fair Oaks could not have been worse for the South. In the days following the *Virginia*'s unsuccessful attempt to break the Union blockade, overall Union commander George B. McClellan landed one hundred thirty thousand Federal soldiers, fourteen thousand horses, and three hundred cannons on the tip of the Yorktown Peninsula, marched them within six miles of Richmond, and now had the Confederate capital city almost completely surrounded. McClellan's troops were camped so close they could hear the Richmond church bells go off on Sunday morning. If that wasn't enough, there was also a second, equally massive force of Union soldiers garrisoning Washington, DC, just ninety miles northeast of Richmond. The Confederacy was about to be crushed by two incomprehensibly gigantor military forces bent on its destruction.

Opposing this onslaught was a ragtag band of fifty thousand demoralized Confederate troops who had just watched their commander beef it off a horse and knock himself out. They were poorly equipped, hungry, exhausted, and outnumbered three to one by a well-supplied force of hardened troops packing top-of-the-line gear, an unquenchable thirst for Rebel blood, and the motive, means, and opportunity to spill plenty of it.

What happened next is the reason why Joseph E. Johnston's replacement—General Robert E. Lee—is now regarded as one of the most brilliant military commanders ever produced on American soil.

The son of former Virginia governor and famous Revolutionary War cavalry commander Harry "Light Horse" Lee, Robert Edward Lee was a thirty-year veteran of the US military who was so famous for his tactical brilliance that when the Civil War initially began, Abraham Lincoln had personally offered to make Lee the overall commander of all US military forces. Lee, a native son of Virginia, politely declined—even though he opposed the war, he couldn't lead an army against his fellow Virginians, so he accepted a staff officer position in Richmond. Now, suddenly, he found himself in command of the entire Rebel army on the eastern front.

Lee sprang into action immediately, devising a bold attack plan that nobody saw coming.

Lee knew that his opponent, George McClellan, was a really cautious guy, so he tried to take advantage of that fact. Rather than turtling up and trying to defend the city, Lee took a small number of troops, had them dig trenches in front of Richmond, and then left them there to stare across a battle-field at five full-strength corps of Union infantry, even though such a small force had no chance of survival if the Union attacked. Then he took the main part of his army, crossed the rain-flooded Chickahominy River, and threw the full might of his soldiers at the extreme right flank of the Federal position. Meanwhile, he also sent his A-1 toughest and most daring cavalry commander, Jeb Stuart, all the way around the Union flank to attack their supply and communications depots from the rear. According to Stuart (a swashbuckling cavalryman who wore a cape and an ostrich plume in his hat and carried a nine-shooter revolver with an underbarrel attachment that fired a 10-gauge shotgun charge of buckshot), the only time his Virginia Cavalry stopped during their 150-mile ride was to receive kisses from the local women. He lost one man, got much-needed intel for Lee, cut off the Federals, and made the front page of every newspaper in the South.

Given the strategic situation, you can probably guess that on the morning of June 26, 1862, the Union soldiers of General Fitz John Porter's Federal V Corps really weren't expecting to see tens of thousands of gunslinging Confederate troops come charging out through the rain and mud. Porter's troops put up a good fight, but before long their lines began to buckle. McClel-lan, already hesitant to begin with, lost his nerve, completely panicked, and ordered a retreat. Then over the next seven days of nonstop warfare, Robert E. Lee led the Army of Northern Virginia in eight separate battles, repeatedly pounding the Union where they least expected it. Lee's troops paid dearly for every inch of ground they took, suffering almost twenty thousand casualties in the course of just one calendar week, but amazingly they managed to send the entire Union army reeling. When McClellan tried to move some of his eighty thousand troops up to help Porter's battered corps, Lee ordered the small group of men defending Richmond to charge—not as a stupid suicide attack but as a diversion to keep McClellan guessing about what was going on. Scrambling up muddy hills into Union artillery and firing lines, the Army of Northern Virginia fought, scrapped, and clawed its way back from almost certain destruction. By the end of the Seven Days Battle, the Union was in full retreat.

But Robert E. Lee wasn't out of the woods just yet. As you could probably guess, President Lincoln wasn't all that thrilled that George B. McClellan was currently running for his boats, so he took the fresh, pumped-up troops he had back home in Washington, put them under the command of a guy named John Pope, and sent them to threaten Richmond while Lee was off chasing McClellan around the peninsula.

Lee had to act fast. By this point he was in command of about eighty thousand men in and around Richmond, and they were sandwiched between the ninety thousand men McClellan had camped at Yorktown, southeast of Richmond, and the sixty-two thousand other dudes that Pope had marching down

from the north. If those two forces linked up, it was all over. If he committed his entire army to attacking either of them, he left Richmond unguarded.

So, once again, Lee did something that would give most military tacticians an aneurysm.

He attacked.

Robert E. Lee divided his army in the face of his enemy—one of the top three things you're *never* supposed to do when you're a military commander—and sent just twenty-three thousand soldiers under the now famous Stonewall Jackson (remember him?) north to deal with Pope. Despite knowing they were marching into a hopeless situation, on August 24, 1862, Jackson's men slogged a grueling fifty-four miles in just two days. This was an insane achievement, considering that every man was wearing about fifty pounds of gear and carrying a ten-pound rifle, and most of them were walking barefoot because the Confederacy didn't have enough shoes to go around. They then somehow snuck *behind* Pope's army, and attacked the Union supply depot at Alexandria. Pope, freaking out that the enemy was suddenly behind him, turned around and charged, but Jackson fell back into the woods before Pope could get to him. Pope, a shameless self-promoter whose primary job before the Civil War involved supervising the construction of lighthouses on the Great Lakes, continued running around aimlessly looking for Jackson. As he was doing that, Jeb Stuart's cavalry rode around behind Pope from the other side, attacked

a couple more depots, and ransacked Pope's personal supply tent, stealing thirty-five thousand dollars in cash, Pope's military dress uniform, and a notebook containing complete troop dispositions for the entire battlefront.

Pope, now pantsless, broke, and humiliated, didn't even notice when Robert E. Lee sent another big chunk of his army north to hit the Union force while they were off searching for Jackson. This left Lee just a few men to defend Richmond in case McClellan's ninety thousand troops attacked, but he didn't seem to mind.

Pope finally found Jackson on August 28. Stonewall had

set up his forces around Manassas Junction—the same place where he'd earned his famous nickname—and when Pope came out of the woods, Jackson was ready for him.

Pope's men launched a series of vicious assaults on Jackson's lines, the Union commander hurling waves and waves of his men at the Confederates. Stonewall's men held, however, fighting for almost seven hours, their ammunition so low that at one point Wheat's Tigers had to resort to throwing rocks at the enemy as they advanced. They stood their ground, however, the Union bravely charging at them with everything they had, but before long it looked like the battle would end in a draw—the South held, the Union was exhausted, and it seemed the battle was over.

It was at this point that thirty thousand fresh Confederate troops came marching out of the woods—behind Pope's army.

I'll spare you the gory details. Let's just say it didn't end well for Pope. His army was pulverized and he was fired and exiled to Minnesota, never to be heard from again. McClellan loaded his troops into ships, left the peninsula the next day, and was fired as soon as he got back to Washington. It was time for the Army of the Potomac to regroup and reassess the situation.

It had been just ninety days since Robert E. Lee had taken over. He'd walked into a disaster. Now his Army of Northern Virginia was the only military unit left standing within fifty miles of the Confederate capital.

Gone were the proud hopes, the high aspirations that swelled our bosoms a few days ago....[The army] has strong limbs to march and meet the foe, stout arms to strike heavy blows, brave hearts to dare—but the brains, the brains! Have we no brains to use the arms and limbs and eager hearts with cunning?

—Private William Lusk, US Army

Sharpshooters

Organized, recruited, and trained by New Yorker Hiram Berdan, a mechanical engineer and recreational sport shooter who won the national rifleman competition an amazing fifteen years in a row, Berdan's Sharpshooters were an elite regiment who hold the distinction of being among the first sniper units in history. Dressed in their distinctive all-green uniform, this elite Union regiment of eagle-eyed marksmen was used as scouts, skirmishers, and rear guard troops, but was also heavily engaged as front-line troops against Confederate forces at battles from the Seven Days to Gettysburg. They served with Fitz John Porter's corps at Second Bull Run.

The Second Battle of Bull Run (Second Manassas)

Troops
Union: 70,000

Confederate: 55,000

Casualties
Union: 13,824

Confederate: 8,353

Result
Confederate Victory

Camp Life

**Soldiering is 99 percent boredom
and 1 percent sheer terror.**

—Anonymous private, Army of the Potomac

Whether you were garrisoning a town, manning a fort, or just hunkering down for the winter months, the day-to-day life of a Civil War soldier wasn't exactly made up of fiery explosions, high-speed chases, and nonstop bullet-riddled excitement. In fact, any time the troops weren't actively fighting for their lives or marching toward a battlefield, life was pretty much the most mind-numbingly boring thing this side of a middle school social studies lecture.

A typical day in the life of Civil War soldiers might look something like this: They'd be blasted awake by early-rising bugle players honking out reveille super loudly at dawn (who woke up the rooster-like bugle players is a mystery), then crawl out of their bedrolls and get into their uniforms. Everyone would fall in with their regiments for roll call, then sometimes march to "colors," a ceremony where a team of sergeants would raise the flag over the camp and commanding officers would bark out orders for the day. From there soldiers would head back to their campfires for breakfast, usually consisting of coffee, bread, peanuts, and cornmeal (although a lot of Confederate units couldn't scavenge actual coffee beans, so they'd make some almost-certainly-disgusting homemade coffee-like slurry, using peas and peanuts and God knows what else).

After breakfast, troops would fall back into line for drill, which is kind of like the war version of after-school football practice. Soldiers and officers would march all around the campground working on their unit cohesion, spend time practicing their bayoneting skills on human-shaped burlap sacks stuffed with straw, or head to the firing range with their rifles. Drill was a much more important part of a soldier's life in the early days of the war, sometimes going from eight AM to five PM with just one lunch break in between. But toward the end of the war, when almost everyone was a stone-cold steely-eyed veteran, the time needed for drill became less and less.

After drill, troops were pretty much free to do their own thing. Some guys would pull guard duty or be ordered to gather firewood, food, and clean water to keep the camp running. If they were lucky enough to avoid that, they could spend their evenings writing letters to their families, attending prayer services at the chaplain's tent, or taking a fishing pole down to the creek. If they were near a town, they were free to head in and see what was going on. Even if they were camped out in a field in the middle of nowhere, there were guys called sutlers who would follow the army around with a wagon full of useful stuff like tobacco, socks, and whiskey that troops could buy with their hard-earned cash. Soldiers loved to spend their nights hanging out around the campfire and playing music, singing, telling war stories, or trying their hands at games like dominoes, chess, or checkers. Gambling was illegal in most camps, but that didn't stop guys from betting on card games such as poker or seven-up or on dice games with names like craps and chuck-a-luck. Likewise, it was illegal to get drunk and get into fights, but that didn't keep the guys of the Forty-Fourth Infantry from hitting the moonshine a little too hard and ending up in fistfights with those jerks from the Seventh Artillery.

The Deadliest Day

The Battle of Antietam

Sharpsburg, Maryland ✳ *September 17, 1862*

I regard the death and mangling of a couple
thousand men as a small affair,
a kind of morning dash—and it may be
well that we become so hardened.

—General William Tecumseh Sherman, US Army

ON THE NIGHT OF SEPTEMBER 6, 1862, THE
Army of Northern Virginia camped in Maryland. For the
first time in the war, the South was on the offensive in enemy
territory.

The stakes were high. Having kicked the Yankees' top commanders up and down Northern Virginia, Robert E. Lee knew
that there would be no better time to take the fight to the

North and let the Federals defend their own turf for a change. Not only would an attack on the North take some pressure off Virginia, but the great powers of Europe, intrigued by Rebel victories and in dire need of Southern cotton for their textile factories, were starting to consider maybe getting involved in this little North American showdown.

The Southern states were Europe's primary source of cotton, and by September 1862 Confederate envoys in Britain, Russia, and France were making headway in persuading the great powers across the Atlantic to come to the South's aid, break the Union naval blockade on the Southern states, and force an end to this war. With the British prime minister already sending Abraham Lincoln letters requesting a diplomatic solution "with plans at separation," all the Southerners needed was one decisive victory on Northern soil to prove their worth and seal the deal. The forty thousand ragged, grizzled veteran soldiers of the Army of Northern Virginia had come to claim that victory, win a battle on enemy soil, lay waste to Northern railroad lines, demoralize the population, threaten DC, and put an end to this silly war once and for all.

Unfortunately for them, some absentminded Confederate officer wrapped the entire battle plan for the invasion around three expensive cigars and then promptly lost the bundle in a field somewhere, where a group of elated Federal scouts stumbled across it, passed the orders along to their commanding officer, then smoked the cigars just to add insult to injury.

Luckily for Robert E. Lee, their commanding officer was George B. McClellan, the commander who had bungled the attack on Richmond. McClellan had been fired for incompetence, but when his replacements proved to be even worse than he was, Lincoln had no choice but to call this guy back. Apparently, Lincoln had forgotten that McClellan was a man so overly cautious that it probably took him four hours and eighty thousand soldiers before he'd commit to brushing his teeth in the morning.

George McClellan had, in his hands, a piece of paper handwritten by Robert E. Lee that clearly explained exactly what the Confederate army was going to do. Lee had forty thousand men, but he'd already split them into two groups—three divisions were scattered throughout western Maryland, while Stonewall Jackson's corps was off at Harper's Ferry trying to capture the Federal arsenal there. McClellan had ninety thousand soldiers and knew exactly where the enemy forces were, what they were planning, and how they were laid out.

McClellan had the military equivalent of a cheat code in a video game. It was the sort of thing that any army commander in military history would have gouged out an eye to receive.

Naturally, he proceeded with extreme caution.

On September 14, three corps of McClellan's Army of the Potomac advanced toward South Mountain, looking to wedge themselves between Lee's detachments, split the Confederate forces in half, and potentially annihilate the entire Army of Northern Virginia. All that opposed him was the five thousand men of General D. H. Hill's division. Hill, a cantankerous North Carolina college professor who loved nothing more than a good fight, positioned his Georgians and North Carolinians in a mountain pass called Turner's Gap, dug trenches, armed every man in his unit from the officers down to the cooks and orderlies, and told his toxic force of soon-to-be-doomed soldiers to stand fast, fight to the death, and hold the line because this is Sparta and all that. When he looked out at the sea of blue-uniformed men marching toward his position, Hill later remarked, "I do not remember ever to have experienced a feeling of greater loneliness."

Amazingly, despite a couple of charges by a steel-toed Union army that outnumbered the Confederates twelve to one, Daniel Harvey Hill's division held the pass for most of the day but could not roll back the tide of McClellan's forces. The blue-coated men struggled up the rugged slopes of the mountain, scoring a key victory.

Lee, knowing now that his plans had been discovered, scrambled to consolidate his forces. He pulled his men back to defensive positions around Sharpsburg, called back Hill's men from the Gap, and sent word to Jackson to hurry up with the capture of Harper's Ferry because things just got real around here.

On the fifteenth of September, he had just eighteen thousand active troops to face seventy-five thousand of McClellan's men.

McClellan didn't attack. Lee continued bringing in men from the Ferry to beef up his numbers.

By the time the Army of the Potomac finally got its act together and attacked on the morning of September 17, Lee had brought up most of Stonewall's corps and was now entrenched in defensive positions outside Sharpsburg with twenty-seven thousand men. He was still in trouble, but McClellan had missed a golden opportunity to decimate the enemy troops before they could regroup.

McClellan opened the festivities with a lights-out artillery bombardment on the Confederate left, mowing down the cornfield where Stonewall Jackson's corps were positioned. The Confederates, hoping to conceal themselves among the cornstalks, were ripped to shreds by artillery blasts that clear-cut the stalks, mulching everything in their path and leaving behind nothing but scorched earth. This jumbo barrage of Union artillery deforested the cornfield, forcing Stonewall's men to fall back toward a white church that belonged, ironically enough, to a German parish that was super into nonviolence and peace and not blowing up people with cannonballs.

The barrage was followed by an all-out charge by Fighting Joe Hooker's corps. Fighting Joe, a hard-drinking Massachusetts boy, led his men barreling into Stonewall's shattered units, hoping to overwhelm them.

Stonewall appealed for help. He got John Bell Hood's Texas brigade.

You know the expression "Don't mess with Texas"? That's good advice. John Bell Hood's knife-wielding Texans,

Hood's Texas Brigade
storming through
the cornfield

blood-raged because they'd been called into combat just as they were getting ready to cook their first hot meal in three days, came blitzing out of the Confederate lines into Hooker's corps. Firing their muskets and fighting for everything they were worth, Hood's Texans charged out of the gun smoke, blunted the Union attack, pushed Hooker's men back, and broke their lines, but were then ferociously counterattacked by a second Union corps that came flying in out of nowhere and decimated Hood's troops with a couple of blasts of artillery. Hood ordered a retreat, falling back to Jackson's original position, but his men had done their job—Jackson had regrouped and was holding the line. When John Bell Hood reported to Stonewall that he'd completed his mission, Jackson asked, "Where is your division?" Hood's response: "Dead on the field."

The second Union assault came around midday, at the center of the Confederate position, where D. H. Hill's already depleted troops were lying prone in an old sunken road. Hill ripped fire into the enemy with everything he had, knowing that he was the only thing holding the middle of the Rebel line together. Hill's 2,500 troops, clinging to the narrow sunken road, turned back four separate valiant yet futile assaults by the Union II Corps in under an hour, inflicting nearly one casualty for every Rebel soldier manning the line.

Just as it was looking like the Confederate center would hold out until the apocalypse, one enterprising brigade of New

Yorkers managed to make their way to a ridge overlooking the sunken road, move around to the flank, and immediately open fire right down the line at the exposed Confederate position. The Rebels, caught completely off guard, suddenly found themselves in a shooting gallery that would earn the sunken road the nickname "Bloody Lane." One Confederate brigade commander caught in the middle of the action, General John Brown Gordon, was wounded four times in the fighting, including a bullet that severed an artery in his leg and another that destroyed his arm, but he continued to rally his men until a fifth bullet hit him in the face, knocking him unconscious (he'd survive and become governor of Georgia after the war).

The Rebel center broke, clearing the way toward Sharpsburg, the now freaking-out Confederate commanders doing everything in their power to hold the line against the Union advance. D. H. Hill grabbed a musket off a dead soldier and personally led two hundred men in a charge to retake a position that was being overrun by the Federals. General James Longstreet, second in command of the Confederate army only to Robert E. Lee, rushed to the front and manned a cannon. Times were as desperate as they could get—the Confederates had nothing in reserve, their lines were crumbling, and every single semi-healthy soldier who had come across the Potomac River into Maryland was now currently deployed in the field.

The Rebels were pushed to the breaking point, clinging with their teeth and fingernails. McClellan still had a full reserve corps of infantry—over ten thousand men—in position a mile from the field, waiting to get into the fray, yet once again the overly cautious Union commander refused to send them in to exploit the gap.

Later in the afternoon, the attack began on the Confederate right flank, where Union General Ambrose E. Burnside—the general who'd had so much trouble with Wheat's Tigers at the First Battle of Bull Run—attempted to force his fourteen-thousand-man corps over the narrow stone bridge that spanned Antietam Creek. Burnside's men were concealed in the woods on the Union side, but even though Antietam Creek was so shallow that a man could walk across it without getting his chin wet, for some reason Burnside was determined to cross his entire force over a bridge that was only wide enough for eight soldiers to march side by side.

All that opposed Burnside was 450 Georgians under the command of former US senator Robert Toombs. Toombs's small unit was hidden in the trees on a big hill overlooking the bridge, dug in with excellent cover on high ground, and all their guns and cannons were ranged in to pick off anyone who set foot on the bridge, but even so this wasn't exactly an ideal situation. However, despite the entire rest of their division being called away to reinforce Confederate positions at Bloody Lane and the cornfield, Toombs's men stood their ground, battling for everything they were worth and pouring fire on the stone bridge that would come to be known as Burnside's Bridge.

Amazingly, the Georgians held the bridge for several hours, scouring the Federals with bullets any time they set foot in the open. Burnside, a man whose fiancée said "no" and ran away crying when the priest asked "Do you take this man" at his wedding (the woman, Lottie Moon, ended up working as a spy for the Confederacy), finally had enough of seeing his people get shot to shreds, so he assembled two of his harshest fighting units—the Fifty-First Pennsylvania Infantry and the Fifty-First New York Infantry—and told them he was going to double their whiskey rations if they could take that bridge and I mean right stinking now, gentlemen.

The two units fixed bayonets, ran for it, braved a hostile spray of bullets, shrapnel, and artillery, forced their way across the bridge despite heavy casualties, lowered their bayonet-equipped rifles, and charged up the hill at the Georgians who had terrorized their brethren. The survivors of Toombs's command split out of there (the other half lay dead).

For some ungodly reason, with the entire Confederate flank destroyed and an undefended Sharpsburg sitting there for the taking, General Ambrose E. Burnside ordered the Fifty-First New York and Pennsylvania not to pursue. He then spent the next two hours (!) crossing the rest of his men over that same stupid bridge and forming them up on the other side.

Right around the time he was ready to move, Burnside's men saw a huge force of men marching toward them in blue uniforms, flying American flags. Burnside was like, what the heck is going on, then watched in horror as this new unit lowered their rifles, and opened fire at point-blank range, cutting a gaping hole into Burnside's ranks.

It was Confederate general Ambrose Powell Hill's division of battle-hardened Rebels, fresh off a seventeen-mile march from Harper's Ferry, decked out in uniforms and equipment they'd just looted from the Federal arsenal. Burnside's inexperienced troops fell back to the bridge and failed to press the attack.

The fighting had been gruesome, and Lee had almost broken three times under the relentless Federal assault, but in the end the decimated Army of Northern Virginia somehow held the line. The next day, both forces were stuck in a staring contest. McClellan naturally didn't want to attack. Lee did, but he knew he didn't have the manpower. Lee waited until nightfall, then slipped his Army of Northern Virginia back across the river and out of Maryland. McClellan refused to give chase to Lee's decimated army.

This was the last straw as far as President Lincoln was concerned. The commander in chief stripped McClellan of his command for the second time and promoted Ambrose Burnside, of all people, to lead the Army of the Potomac instead. McClellan responded by returning home and preparing to run against Abraham Lincoln in the presidential election of 1864 under a platform of "Hey, let's stop fighting this war because it's stupid."

The Battle of Antietam was the single bloodiest day not only of the Civil War but in all of American military history. The horrifying carnage left twenty-three thousand casualties, a number that is more than the Americans who died in the Revolutionary War, the War of 1812, the Mexican-American War, and the Spanish-American War *combined*. It's over nine times the number of Americans killed at D-day.

Technically, the battle is considered a draw, but it was a strategic Union victory. The Union failed to destroy Lee, and Lee failed to win a history-altering victory on Union territory, but the consequences of Antietam were even more wide-ranging than that—it was the deciding factor in Europe's refusal to throw their support behind the Southern cause. If the South was going to win the war, it was going to have to do it without any outside help.

Photographic Memory

One of the world's first photojournalists, New Yorker Mathew Brady used the relatively new technology of the photograph to take some of the most intense pictures of the Civil War. Following the armies around on the front lines and using a covered wagon as a makeshift darkroom while bombs exploded around them, Brady and his team of photographers took over 3,500 pictures of the conflict, documenting the Civil War in a way that no other war to date had ever been recorded. These photos not only provided families lasting memories of their sons, brothers, and husbands but also enabled newspapers and magazines to bring the horrors of war into the living room of every person in the country.

The Angel of the Battlefield

A Massachusetts schoolteacher with no medical training, Clara Barton, "the Angel of the Battlefield," volunteered to work as a nurse at dozens of engagements. At Antietam, she was so close to the fighting that one of the men she was assisting was killed as she was working on him, the bullet passing through the sleeve of her dress and hitting him in the heart. Barton would follow the Army of the Potomac with wagonloads of medical supplies, aiding wounded men wherever she came across them. She would end up founding the American Red Cross after the war, serving as its president from 1882 to 1904, and dedicating her life to identifying anonymous soldiers killed in action.

West Point

One important thing to take into account when reading daring tales of heroic generals battling one another is that most of these men knew each other, and many of them had gone to college together. For instance, while A. P. Hill was an upperclassman at

West Point, he tried to steal the fiancée of his roommate, George McClellan. McClellan responded by telling his fiancée a bunch of horrible lies about Hill, and married Mary Ellen McClellan in 1854.

Confederate general A. P. Hill

The Battle of Antietam

Troops
Union: 87,000
Confederate: 45,000

Casualties
Union: 12,401
Confederate: 10,316

Result
Union Victory

Chancellorsville

Jackson and Lee's Finest Hour

*The Wilderness, Virginia * May 1–3, 1863*

> Always mystify, mislead, and surprise the enemy, if possible; and when you strike and overcome him, never let up in the pursuit so long as your men have strength to follow; for an army routed, if hotly pursued, becomes panic-stricken, and can then be destroyed by half their number. The other rule is, never fight against heavy odds, if by any possible maneuvering you can hurl your own force on only a part, and that the weakest part, of your enemy and crush it. Such tactics will win every time, and a small army may thus destroy a large one in detail, and repeated victory will make it invincible.
>
> —Stonewall Jackson

THOMAS J. "STONEWALL" JACKSON WAS as tough a human being as was ever produced in the United States: a hardened, seemingly emotionless, vicious killing machine who thought of nothing but outmaneuvering the enemy, striking swiftly and destroying him utterly and without mercy. This is a man who, in response to one of his subordinate officers lamenting the destruction of thousands of brave Yankees who had just been mowed down charging Stonewall's position, said, "No. Shoot them all. I do not wish them to be brave."

A stern, blue-eyed killer, Stonewall was super religious, ruthless, and incredibly eccentric. He never ate pepper because he thought it made his leg hurt. He always walked around with one arm in the air because that was the only way he could keep himself balanced. He didn't drink because he "liked it too much." He never mailed a letter that would be in transit on a Sunday, because that was the Lord's day of rest. At almost any point during a battle, he could be found sucking on a lemon. But this guy was hardcore. A veteran of four battles during the Mexican-American War, he continued to stand unflinching as bullets whizzed past his head when he had a finger shot off during the First Bull Run, calmly telling one of his men, "God has fixed the time for my death. I do not concern myself about that, but to always be ready, no matter when it may overtake me. Captain, that is the way all men should live, and then all would be equally brave."

We've already seen big things from him. Facing the full might of the Union charge at Bull Run, Jackson responded by earning his famous nickname, Stonewall. In the Shenandoah Valley in 1862, he marched his men six hundred miles and won twelve consecutive battles, driving the Union out of the region. At the Second Bull Run he humiliated Federal general John Pope so ruthlessly it ended the man's military career. At Antietam, he withstood a direct assault by forces that had him ranged in with every piece of artillery they had.

Chancellorsville, however, would surpass all of his previous accomplishments. It would also be his final battle.

Following the horrific carnage at Antietam, Union commander George McClellan refused to pursue Lee's army as it retreated back to Virginia, so Lincoln replaced him with Ambrose Burnside, the dude who had failed to destroy the Tigers at Bull Run and who couldn't successfully cross a one-hundred-foot-long bridge at Antietam despite outnumbering his opposition by a factor of a hundred. Burnside, being Burnside, naturally took the entire Army of the Potomac into Northern Virginia, found Lee camped at Fredericksburg with a ton of artillery and his men entrenched behind a bulletproof stone wall, and ordered his troops to run up a supersteep hill straight into the barrels of the Confederate artillery cannons. The charge was obliterated. So Burnside ordered them to do it again. And again. And again.

He lost twelve thousand men in six separate assaults, none of which accomplished anything. He was understandably fired.

Lincoln then appointed Fighting Joe Hooker, a Seminole War and Mexican-American War veteran who spent much of his nonfighting time talking about how useless Burnside was. Hooker, a man who liked drinks and women and fighting so much it was part of his nickname, found himself in command of 130,000 men and four hundred cannons, staring across the battlefield at just sixty thousand Rebels who were so undersupplied that they had no shoes and were wearing uniforms their moms stitched for them.

"My plan is perfect," Hooker reported to Lincoln in a letter. And, honestly, it kind of was. First, Hooker revamped the Union cavalry to make it less useless, then ordered it to ride around the Confederate flank Jeb Stuart–style, burning and raiding supply lines to mess up Lee's mojo and force him to send his own troops to do something about it. Then Hooker kept one part of his force at Fredericksburg, but instead of attacking, he left them there to hold Lee's army in place. Then, while Lee was occupied with that, Hooker marched three corps of infantry fifty-six miles through a dense, horrible tangle of swamp and forest known as the Wilderness, surrounded Lee completely, and patiently waited for Lee to run for it so he could draw him out of his defensive positions and kill him in the open.

The perfect plan was executed perfectly. Hooker was so certain this was the end of the line for the Rebellion that he wrote a letter to Lincoln saying, "The Confederate army is now the legitimate property of the Army of the Potomac.... The enemy must either ingloriously fly or come out from behind his defenses and give us battle upon our own ground, where certain destruction awaits him." Hooker was already planning what he was going to wear during the victory parade when he came home as a hero.

Except Lee didn't run. He attacked. Just not where Hooker was expecting it.

Lee had perfect intel on enemy positions, thanks again to Jeb Stuart, and in yet another example of the genius that was Robert E. Lee, the Confederate commander ordered just one division—ten thousand men—to stay at Fredericksburg and hold the line against forty thousand Federals, while he took the rest of them and moved them through the Wilderness.

Then he split his army again. He left twenty thousand men to face ninety thousand, then sent Stonewall Jackson off through the Wilderness to try to flank the enemy.

For the record, this is insanity. Dividing your army *twice* while facing a force that outnumbers you two to one is the sort of tactic that would get most people laughed out of the military academy. Jackson's supply train was six miles long, and he needed to march them twelve miles silently through an impenetrable forest, hit the enemy from the rear, and do it all without Fighting Joe Hooker figuring out what was going on, because if Hooker had any idea what was happening, he could potentially have ended the Civil War in one single attack.

Hooker did receive word that the enemy was on the move. He was just so confident of victory that he assumed they were running away, so he ordered his men to stand fast.

At five PM on May 2, 1863, the men of Union major general Oliver O. Howard's division were camped on the extreme flank of the Union army, just chilling in camp, cooking their dinner, joking and talking about whether or not they were going to see any action the next morning.

Then a stampede of rabbits and deer came scampering out of the woods to Howard's right. They were followed by twenty-five thousand Southerners. Men who had marched nine hours through dense forest, their clothes ripped apart by branches and brambles, screaming, frothing at the mouth, firing their rifles, and running full speed into the astonished Federals. According to Howard, "The attacking force emerged from the forest and rushed on....The men in front would halt and fire, and while these were reloading, another set would run before them, halt and fire, in no regular line, but in such multitudes that our men went down before them like trees in a hurricane."

The Federals, many of whom didn't even have their rifles within reach, just dropped their bacon and ran for it. Men, carts, mules, and horses clogged the only road out of there, making them easy pickings for Jackson's battle-raging men. Union troops attempted to regroup, but in the confusion many units crashed into one another, artillery batteries fired on their own men, and it was basically chaos.

Jackson pushed his attack until dark, liquidating the entire flank of Hooker's army, forcing the Yankees to fall back

to defensive positions, and dramatically throwing a monkey wrench into Hooker's "perfect plan."

Unfortunately for Jackson, as he was returning to camp from surveying the damage he'd just created, pickets from the Eighteenth North Carolina Infantry accidentally mistook him for a Union cavalry raider and opened fire, hitting their commanding officer with three bullets. He was rushed from the field, had his left arm amputated, and was dead a few days later.

But the battle still wasn't over. Hooker's men regrouped, and the Army of the Potomac was still holding more men in reserve than Lee had in his entire army. Hooker, who'd understandably kind of lost his nerve a little bit, ordered his men to pull back, but Lee wasn't about to let him off the hook. Jackson's corps, now under the command of Jeb Stuart, pressed them hard, firing artillery shells that set the forest on fire and burned hundreds of Union troops to death. Then, just to add insult to injury, a cannonball hit Hooker's headquarters building, knocking the building down on top of him (he lived). With Lee moving in to capture the Federals in a pocket, Hooker ordered a full withdrawal.

Back at Fredericksburg, the Union commander, "Uncle John" Sedgwick, realized he had to do something. Sedgwick, a Connecticut boy, recognized the importance of the situation—Hooker's army was in full retreat, pursued by the

Confederates, and if he didn't do something, the entire Army of the Potomac could be annihilated.

So he attacked Fredericksburg.

Think about this for a second—Uncle John Sedgwick, with just one corps of infantry (the rest of his detachment had been called away to assist Hooker), was about to attack a position that had just cost Ambrose Burnside an entire army.

Well, Sedgwick had a simple theory—Burnside was a wuss. Uncle John assembled his men, explained that the fate of the Union hinged on this attack, and ordered them not to screw around with firing, loading their rifles, or stopping for anything ever. Just attach their bayonets, get their knickers up that hill as fast as they could, and stab any face that popped up out of the earthworks once they got there.

His men got it done. Uncle John Sedgwick's Yankees rushed uphill into the heart of the enemy formations, dove into the trenches, and broke the Rebel defenses at extreme close range. They took one thousand prisoners, captured fifteen pieces of artillery, and overran the field, turning Lee's flank in the process. The Confederate commander had no choice but to call off his attack on Hooker's retreating forces and redirect his troops to shore up the position. Once his job was complete, Sedgwick withdrew through the fog during the night of May 4, getting back to friendly lines with the rest of his men.

The Battle of Chancellorsville had cost Fighting Joe

Hooker seventeen thousand men and was such an unbelievable victory for the South that the fight is now studied in basically every military academy in the world. Naturally, Hooker
was fired when he returned to Washington, the fifth commander of the Army of the Potomac to be canned in the last
two years (sixth if you count McClellan being sacked twice).

Victory once again bolstered the Army of Northern Virginia's feelings of invincibility, but the victory was bittersweet,
as it came at the cost of Stonewall Jackson. The Confederate
army would never be the same again.

The Biggest Killer

The most common cause of death in the Civil War wasn't bullets or artillery—it was disease. Thanks to terrible living conditions in filthy camps, long marches through insect-infested swamps, substandard drinking water, and close-quarters transmission of infectious diseases, over 61 percent of fatalities in the war were brought on by a series of ailments that ran rampant through the camps on both sides. Dysentery, typhoid, malaria, tuberculosis, and the ambiguous disease known as "camp fever" were common killers across the board, bringing even the toughest soldiers to their knees, but brave men met their ends at the hands of everything from measles and smallpox to scurvy and diarrhea. (Yikes.)

The Draft

In 1863, the Federal government instituted a draft, requiring every man of military age to either enlist in the military or "donate" three hundred dollars to the war effort. This didn't go over well in New York, which broke out into a weeklong series of riots beginning on July 13, 1863. The rioters, mostly Irish immigrants and low-wage laborers, set fire to the recruiting office, destroyed trolley tracks and telegraph wires, and took out their frustrations on local blacks, whom they blamed for the war. A police station was destroyed, the colonel of the Eleventh New York Infantry was shot trying to stop the rioting, and dozens of black men were beaten and killed in the streets. Over a million dollars' worth of damage was done to the city, 120 people were killed, and another 120 were wounded before Federal troops and Catholic priests finally put an end to the mayhem.

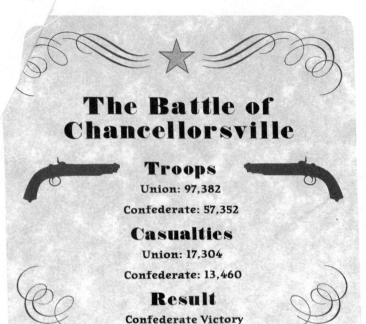

The Battle of Chancellorsville

Troops
Union: 97,382

Confederate: 57,352

Casualties
Union: 17,304

Confederate: 13,460

Result
Confederate Victory

Chancellorsville battle re-creation

Horse and Steel

The Battle of Brandy Station

*Culpepper County, Virginia * June 9, 1863*

Who can describe the feelings of a man on entering a charge? How exhilarating, and yet how awful. The glory of success in a charge is intoxicating! One forgets everything, even personal safety, in the grand thought of vanquishing the enemy. We were in for it now, and the nerves were strung to the highest tension.

—Lieutenant R. B. Porter, First Maine Cavalry

THE THUNDEROUS SOUND OF THOUSANDS OF horse hooves trampling the earth beneath them rumbled across the Federal battle lines as the men of the First Maine Cavalry re-formed their battle line, their eyes fixed forward at the Sixth Virginia Cavalry regiment and the battalion of heavy horse-drawn artillery lining the body-strewn ridge above them.

As their bugler blared the command to charge, the men quickened their pace, spurring their steeds on at the gallop with a yell as they prepared to run full-bore into the enemy lines. Those men who still had ammunition in their six-shooters tried to steady their weapons as they bulldozed their way toward the rattle of enemy muskets, while others simply unsheathed the tried-and-true weapon of old-school horse-mounted destruction—their gleaming, curved steel sabers.

Several massive clouds of smoke appeared on the ridge as the Maine cavalry galloped ahead, the sight of the cannon's firing reaching them well before the deafening boom. The air whistled menacingly as razor-sharp, white-hot shards of shrapnel ripped into the cavalry's ranks, sending horses and men crumpling to the earth in a heap with about the same velocity as a guy driving a motorcycle into a brick wall at thirty-five miles an hour without a helmet.

Those men still in the saddle didn't lose a step. The death screams of their friends just hardened their resolve. When they reached the Confederate lines, those artillerymen would pay.

The First Maine was an unlikely group of horsemen. Recruited from lumberjacks, machinists, fishermen, and New England dockworkers, the unit had been organized just a few months earlier. Most of the guys only recently learned how to ride a horse. Now they suddenly found themselves making their first-ever cavalry charge right in the middle of the largest cavalry battle in American history. Twenty thousand men on

horseback battled one another in a swirling, sword-swinging melee across a rolling grassy plain in an epic death match that had more in common with medieval knightly combat than anything resembling modern warfare.

The First Maine crashed into the Sixth Virginia with all their weight, horse smashing against horse and sabers colliding so hard they generated sparks and dented steel. Troopers emptied their revolvers into the enemy, swung their blades with ruthless efficiency, and, in some cases, grabbed enemy riders and pulled them from their horses, both troopers falling to the ground, grappling like wrestlers as horses stampeded past them in every direction. Caught in the middle were the artillery gunners, still struggling to reload their cannons. Some of the artillerymen fought back by swinging their ramrods like clubs. Others ran. The rest were hacked to pieces.

With a mighty cheer, the Federal cavalry raised their sabers high as the shattered remnants of the Sixth Virginia withdrew, leaving the First Maine in command of the ridge. Their joy, however, would be short-lived—no sooner did they see the enemy withdraw than a battle line of the Eleventh Virginia Cavalry galloped to the aid of their artillery, their sabers gleaming in the June sun, their pistols leveled and loaded.

The First Maine drew up in a defensive position, gritted their teeth, and prepared for battle once again.

There was much more on the line here than simply a battery of cannons and possession of a meaningless hill. Just two miles from the battlefield lay the entirety of Robert E. Lee's Army of Northern Virginia—almost sixty thousand men, fresh off their unparalleled victory at Chancellorsville, camped on the banks of the Rappahannock River in preparation for a second full-scale invasion of the Northern states. The Confederate cavalry, led by the now infamous Jeb Stuart, was supposed to be screening this force, keeping their location hidden from the Federals, but instead of performing much-needed reconnaissance, Jeb staged a huge cavalry review to impress all the chicks of Culpepper, Virginia, and failed to notice an entire corps of Union cavalry assembling across the river on the other side.

Up until this point in the war, the Federal cavalry had more or less been a total joke. Stuart and his Virginia cavalry had ridden around their entire army *twice*, stolen their commander's clothes, defeated them in battle countless times, destroyed depots deep behind their lines, and basically just made them look like a bunch of fools. But that was about to change.

Realizing that he had, for the first time in the entire war, finally got the drop on the Confederates, Union commander Fighting Joe Hooker ordered his cavalry to "disperse or destroy" the Rebel cavalry. So, in the pitch darkness at four thirty in the morning on June 9, 1863, five thousand cavalry troopers under General John Buford forded the Rappahannock River and charged out of the fog toward the Rebel lines, meeting Confederate sentries with their guns blazing. At the sound of gunfire the Confederates, not expecting a fight, scrambled out of their beds, hopped on their horses, and rushed into the woods to see what was going on. The men of the Sixth and Seventh Virginia, many of them fighting in their underwear, with no boots, riding bareback on their horses, flew toward the enemy, firing their carbines and pistols through the darkness and fog at the sounds of battle, unaware that they were actually facing three full regiments of Union cavalry in a full-on attack.

In the confusion and destruction that followed, Buford's second-in-command, Benjamin "Grimes" Davis, was killed in action, shot in the head at close range while swinging his saber in one hand and holding his Colt pistol in the other. His command, the Eighth New York, Eighth Illinois, and Third Indiana, continued on, breaking through the Virginians and pushing them back to hastily constructed defenses at the top of a hill near a church.

Atop the hill were five brigades of cavalry and twenty cannons under the command of an unlikable Confederate commander known as "Grumble" Jones. Grumble, whose nickname came from his not-so-sunny disposition (he'd been in a bad mood ever since 1852, when his newlywed bride was ripped from his arms in a shipwreck and drowned), was permanently angry and disliked even by his own troops, but he was also always ready for a fight. When he heard things going down, he managed to throw his troops in a line atop the hill, where they'd have excellent lines of fire on anything coming his way.

But Buford wasn't about to stop just because there were a couple dozen cannons pointed in his direction. He ordered the Federals to take the hill.

Leading the charge was the Sixth Pennsylvania Cavalry, a regiment that traced its history to George Washington's personal bodyguard during the American Revolution. Known as Rush's Lancers, the Sixth Pennsylvania was famous for carrying nine-foot-long wood-and-steel lances—medieval knight–style—into battle. By 1863, most of the troopers had ditched these unwieldy ancient contraptions for something more useful (that is, hopefully something that actually fired a bullet or other such projectile). If nothing else, this detail should give you the basic idea of what was going on with this regiment—these Pennsylvania boys were looking to get dirty and duke it out with the Rebels, and they weren't about to back down in the face of murderous artillery fire.

The Sixth Pennsylvania charged the hill in perfect order even as canister fire and shrapnel scythed through their ranks, cutting men down like grass under a lawn mower. The Pennsylvanians continued straight ahead, leveling their sabers at the enemy, crashing into his lines, and going after him with sword points and pistol muzzles. The attack pushed the Virginians back, but Grumble Jones managed to retake the hill. Buford then attempted a flanking maneuver, sending the Second Massachusetts and the Third Wisconsin Infantry around the side of the church, where they successfully overran a detachment of dismounted Rebel cavalrymen who had taken up positions behind a stone wall, both sides swarming against each other, swinging their rifles like clubs and stabbing with bayonets and knives.

It was at this point that overall Confederate cavalry commander Jeb Stuart, watching from the top of a hill about a mile from the battlefield, nearly jumped out of his skin at the sound of gunfire *right behind him.*

He looked out the window of his headquarters building to see 2,800 Federal horsemen emerging from the forest just a couple hundred yards from his location, guns blazing. Fighting Joe Hooker had sent a second detachment to cross the Rappahannock six miles south and surprise Jeb from the rear.

It almost worked.

As Stuart scrambled to order troops back from the front to assist, all that stood between the Confederate commander and an untimely demise was a lowly lieutenant named John Carter and the single six-pound cannon he'd brought back from the battlefield to resupply and refit. When he saw the Union closing in, Carter grabbed the gun, by himself, and sprinted up the hill, dragging it behind him in a desperate race to reach the top of Fleetwood Hill before the Federals, knowing full well that he had only enough black powder to fire one shot.

Despite all odds, Carter reached the top of the hill, sighted the gun at the enemy, stuffed in the black powder, rammed in some metal shavings, a handful of bullets, and a chain (he didn't have any shells), and fired.

His shot missed badly, but the Federals, thinking they were facing an entire battery of Confederate artillery and not just some random dude with a handful of nails and access to explosives, halted their disorganized march, took cover, and spent the next couple of minutes forming up for a full-scale, organized charge up the hill. By the time they launched their attack, Jeb Stuart's fastest riders were already starting to get into position atop Fleetwood Hill.

The Union regiments blitzed ahead, undeterred by the enemy forces opposing them, their resolve hardened to settle the score with cold steel and piping-hot gun barrels. The Rebel cavalry was ready for it.

The Battle for Fleetwood Hill was one of the last true cavalry melees in military history. At a time when technology had advanced to the point of Gatling guns, submarines, and six-shooter pistols, the next five hours of battle were a disorganized mess more akin to something out of the Crusades than a modern war. Warriors on horseback rode hard against one another, the battle lines intermingling in a swirling, fluid battle as old-school sword fights were intertwined with .44-caliber pistol bullets in a chaos of heroism and carnage. The Sixth New York Artillery rolled their guns right into the middle of the fight, blasting canister shot into horse and men alike, knowing that nearly every man in the unit would die with his guns.

The battle went back and forth, both sides taking, losing, and then retaking Fleetwood Hill. The high point came when the First Maine, making their first charge of the war, broke the Sixth Virginia and overran an artillery position, then fought bravely against the Eleventh Virginia before finally being forced to withdraw from the hill.

Rebel reinforcements dispatched from Lee's main army began to arrive around five PM, and the Federal cavalry, exhausted, depleted, and virtually out of ammunition after nearly twelve hours of nonstop combat, withdrew from the field. Even though they'd suffered heavy losses and failed to discover Lee's army, kill Stuart, or hold the field, they'd made their point—Yankee cavalry wasn't lying down and letting Jeb Stuart ride his horses all over them. For the first time, they'd managed to surprise Stuart (and do it twice in the same day) and put up a fight against him.

It wouldn't be the last the Army of Northern Virginia would hear from the Federal cavalry.

Civil War Cuisine

Food in the Civil War was terrible. It consisted of meat, bread, dehydrated vegetables, salt, coffee, whiskey, sugar, dried peas, peanuts, and cornmeal, which doesn't sound so bad, except that there was no refrigeration or canned food or shrink-wrap or Ziploc bags during this time period, and on the occasions when you could actually get food to you and weren't stuck foraging in the woods for stuff, it was pretty much all rotten and mealy and infested with worms and bugs. The standard meal of the Union was something called hardtack—an incredibly unappetizing cracker-like brick of flour and salt that was just as likely to chip a tooth as it was to be digested properly. In the South, they had johnnycakes, which is a cute name for a congealed cornmeal mass packed together with bacon grease that was equally effective as food as it was as an instrument for hand-to-hand combat.

Name Game

Confederate cavalry commander William Henry Fitzhugh Lee, Robert E. Lee's son and future congressman from Virginia, should not be confused with Confederate cavalry commander Fitzhugh Lee, Robert's nephew and the future governor of Virginia. Got it?

Oh, Behave!

Discipline was maintained in camp much in the same way it is in a classroom—with humiliating punishments for people who messed up. For instance, if you were in a cavalry regiment and you slept through morning drill, you had to spend a couple of hours sitting on the *beau sabreur*—a giant stupid-looking wooden horse set up right in the middle of camp—and any time someone from your regiment walked past you they could point and laugh. An infantryman who got too drunk and rowdy would have to ride out his hangover by stripping to his underwear and walking around camp with his arms, legs, and head sticking out of a giant barrel with the word DRUNK written on it in red paint. Obviously, this is awesome.

Lookouts

Back before drones, satellites, cell phones, and GPS, the only way to know where the enemy was, how many men they had, and whether or not they were actively on their way to kill you was to have actual guys standing around looking for them. Both armies utilized scouts known as pickets for this purpose. Working in teams of two to four men, pickets would be positioned as guards about a half mile in front of the main body of the army. Unable to sleep on duty, they watched day and night for any signs of the enemy, and as soon as they made contact they had to ride as fast as possible back to friendly lines to alert their commanders. It was a thankless, dangerous job, but there was no other way to get it done.

The Battle of Brandy Station

Troops
Union: 11,000

Confederate: 9,500

Casualties
Union: 866

Confederate: 433

Result
Confederate Victory

Gettysburg

The Battle of Gettysburg

July 1–3, 1863 ∗ Gettysburg, Pennsylvania

Stand firm, you boys from Maine, for not once in a century are men permitted to bear such responsibility for freedom and justice, for God and humanity as are now placed upon you.

—Colonel Joshua Lawrence Chamberlain, Twentieth Maine Volunteer Infantry

JUST BEFORE THREE PM ON THE THIRD DAY OF the Battle of Gettysburg, thirteen thousand war-weary, battle-forged Confederate soldiers from the Army of Northern Virginia gazed out through the trees at a wide-open field baking under the blazing heat of the Pennsylvania sun. Wiping the sweat from their eyes, the Rebel troopers rested in the relative safety of a small shady forest and grimly stared out across a mile and a half of certain death. Their eyes were fixed on their

nearly impossible objective: an ominous little hill appropriately known as Cemetery Ridge. Atop the ridge, behind a hazy
cloud of gray-white smoke, a sea of nearly twenty-five thousand blue-uniformed soldiers patiently waited, stacked six deep
behind an impressive, bulletproof wall of stones and rocks. The
Union lines bristled with cannon muzzles and bayonet points,
the soldiers' eyes straining for signs of movement in the forest
beyond.

Despite having their lines assailed by an avalanche of artillery shells and explosives from 152 Confederate cannons for
nearly two hours, the Union cannons still hadn't fired a single
shot. Federal gunners knew they'd need every cannonball for
the battle to come.

The Confederate soldiers realized that what they were
being asked to do was virtually impossible. But Robert E. Lee
had asked them to do the impossible before, and every time
these brave veterans had found a way to get the job done. They
gripped their rifles tighter, clenched their teeth, and prepared to
willingly walk straight through the front door of hell once again.

Drawing his officer's sword from its scabbard with the flour-
ish of a swashbuckling pirate, Confederate general George E.
Pickett broke the eerie silence that was left when the cannons
stopped firing. Swirling his blade high, he shouted, "Up, men,
and to your posts—don't forget today that you are from Old
Virginia!"

With a loud cheer, thirteen thousand Confederates climbed

to their feet, formed a battle line that measured a full mile from one side to the other, and prepared to embark on a charge that would completely change the face of the United States forever.

But let's go back to before this battle even started. By June 1863, things were going pretty well for Robert E. Lee's forces. Big-time, mind-bogglingly impossible Rebel victories at Chancellorsville and Fredericksburg had the Army of Northern Virginia thinking they were pretty much invincible. They'd smashed the Federals in battle after battle, defended Richmond from invasion yet again, and ultimately been responsible for the firings of, like, a half-dozen Federal commanders in just under two years of warfare.

Things weren't going so well out west, however, where war-hardened Union general Ulysses S. Grant was stampeding through Tennessee. Through a series of bold attacks and brilliant maneuvers, Grant was now dangerously close to seizing the Rebel stronghold of Vicksburg on the Mississippi River, a position that absolutely had to be held at all costs. To take some of the pressure off Vicksburg and try to save the Confederacy from being cut in half along the Mississippi, Lee led his ever-victorious soldiers on yet another full-scale invasion of the North, marching up through Maryland into Pennsylvania in June 1863. Lee's plan was to rip up rail lines, cause chaos, and steal valuable supplies from Northern depots, then bypass all the fortifications around Washington, DC, and attack the US capital from the direction Federal commanders least expected: north.

The Yankees had almost discovered Lee's army when they ran into Jeb Stuart at Brandy Station, but once the Army of Northern Virginia crossed the border, neither side really knew exactly where the other was. Lee tried to sweep around from the north, and the Federals tried to make sure they stayed between Lee and Washington, DC, but both sides were just kind of feeling around, trying to figure out what was going in.

The two armies met by accident on July 1, 1863, in the small, wildly obscure town of Gettysburg, Pennsylvania. The story goes that Confederate soldiers under A. P. Hill had marched into town because they'd heard there was a sweet shoe factory they could plunder. But as cool as it might be to think that the biggest battle ever fought in North America was the result of some barefoot dude looking for new kicks, that probably wasn't what actually happened. Regardless, Hill's men ended up in Gettysburg for some reason, where they ran into a Federal recon force under the command of a hard-fighting Illinois boy named John Buford. Buford's First Cavalry Division was outnumbered pretty badly, but Buford was a straight-up Sioux-fighting warrior with a sweet mustache, and he wasn't about to back away from an opportunity to shove a rifle in the face of some uppity Southerners who dared set foot on Northern soil. And his First Cavalry troopers were up to the challenge, since they were armed with some brand-spanking-new Sharps rifles that were way more accurate and that reloaded way faster than the traditional muskets Hill's guys were packing.

Buford deployed his troops in a line, and they opened fire on Hill's infantry. When Robert E. Lee and the Federal commander, a guy named George Meade, heard the gunshots, they started sending men to Gettysburg to see what the heck was going on.

The most important battle in American history was on.

Buford held the line for a while but ultimately had to fall back as the Confederates brought more and more soldiers into the mix throughout the day. He was reinforced by Federal troops, including a division commanded by Abner Doubleday (the man who is rumored to have invented baseball, but probably didn't). Ultimately, the Union troops had to fall back and take up positions along Cemetery Ridge just outside of town.

Eighty-five thousand Union soldiers were positioned on Cemetery Ridge, with their flanks anchored on two hills—Culp's Hill on one side and a big, forested hill called Little Round Top on the other. Opposing them were sixty-five thousand Confederates, who were chomping with the realization that they were one epic victory away from smashing the Federal army. They would then capture Washington, DC, and bring the war to a sudden, destructive end that would result in the permanent separation of the United States of America into two countries.

When the sun rose on July 2, Robert E. Lee ordered his

army to launch simultaneous attacks on Culp's Hill and Little Round Top. Unfortunately for him, the attack on Culp's Hill was to be carried out by Stonewall Jackson's corps, which was now commanded by a mostly useless general named Richard Ewell. This guy went by the amazingly unflattering nickname of Old Baldy and really only got around to fighting when he felt like it. At Gettysburg, Ewell sat around all day long, launched a weak attack right around sunset, and accomplished nothing of value. As an interesting side note, Union Army of the Potomac commander George Meade's horse was also named Old Baldy. Meade was referred to as a "damned old goggle-eyed snapping turtle," which proves that there are actually worse nicknames than Old Baldy.

All the serious action on day two of the battle took place on the Little Round Top side of the field, where cigar-chomping New York general Dan Sickles was fighting for his life against a crushing onslaught of Southern warriors. Bloody engagements took place in a wheat field, an orchard of peach trees, and a weird clump of giant gray boulders known as Devil's Den that kind of looks like the landscape of an alien planet. Both sides heroically braved nightmarish fields of raking gunfire, attempting to seize enemy positions, advance, shatter the opposing forces, and defend their gains, only to be knocked back by an onrushing detachment of fresh reinforcements. For hours, troops fought one another like demons at close range, stepping over the bodies of men and horses as bullets buzzed through the air from every direction. The battle was so gruesome that at one point the First Minnesota Infantry had to be sacrificed to cover Sickles's withdrawal. The ultrabrave Minnesotans didn't hesitate as they bayonet-charged a force twice their size in a valiant effort to prevent their position from being buried in gray-jacketed Secessionists. They took on an entire Rebel corps by themselves and suffered 82 percent casualties.

During the battle, General Sickles got his leg blown off by a cannonball, but that iron-jawed New Yorker just calmly hobbled over, picked up his leg and the cannonball that had removed it, and ultimately donated both of them to the National Museum of Health and Medicine (where, weirdly enough, they can still be seen today). As Sickles's men fell back to Cemetery Ridge, they were pumped up and inspired by the sight of their freshly mangled commanding officer calmly smoking a cigar as he was carted off the field in a stretcher.

Sickles withdrew to Cemetery Ridge, and as Rebel troops under John Bell Hood and Evander Law broke through Devil's Den, they were greeted by a very welcome sight: In all the confusion of battle, the Union had accidentally left Little Round Top completely undefended! If the Rebels could get up there and hold that position, they'd have a clear line of fire right down the Union lines. Taking that hill would turn the Union flank, break their army, and sweep away the only thing standing between Robert E. Lee and Abraham Lincoln's Oval Office.

The Rebels made a run for the top of the hill.

General George Meade, commanding the Army of the Potomac, immediately saw what was going on. He gathered the first unit he could find—his reserve troops, who were being held back as a last resort—and sent them sprinting up the hill.

The Union won the race to the top. At the extreme end of the line, 360 soldiers of the Twentieth Maine Volunteer Infantry scraped together some makeshift cover out of a few old boulders and prepared to single-handedly defend the flank of the Union army from a full-scale charge by hardened Confederate troops.

The commander of the Twentieth Maine was a mild-mannered college professor named Joshua Lawrence Chamberlain, who had just ten minutes to prepare his troops for what was to come. But he took the time to calmly (and correctly) remind his forces that the entire fate of the Civil War hinged on what they would accomplish in the next hour of battle. Minutes later, the boys from Maine peered out through the dense forest below to see a horde of gray-clad soldiers charging up toward them, bayonets fixed, weapons at the ready.

For the next hour and a half, the Twentieth Maine and the Fifteenth Alabama fought viciously, intensely, and without mercy. Four times the men of Alabama—who had already marched twenty miles that morning to get to the battlefield—ran up the wooded slopes of Little Round Top, shrieking their Rebel yells as Federal bullets chopped up the trees and vegetation around

them. Loading and firing with clinical precision and contained fury, the men from Maine unloaded blast after blast of gunfire at the attackers, sometimes at point-blank range. On a couple of occasions, the Alabamans reached the Union lines, only to be hurled back by desperate soldiers swinging canteens and ammo packs as weapons and clubbing ferociously with the backs of their rifles.

Finally, after forcing back four separate charges, the Alabamans withdrew down the hill to regroup for one more attack. Chamberlain surveyed his command. Of his original 360 men, only a hundred could still fight. And of the hundred, only a few actually had bullets left. He was out of ammo, his men were exhausted, and in the smoke-covered darkness below, he could hear the Rebels organizing their next fierce assault.

So Joshua Lawrence Chamberlain, the mild-mannered teacher, decided to do something so over-the-top insane that it just might work.

He ordered his men to fix bayonets and prepare to charge.

When the Fifteenth Alabama made their sixth exhausting run up to capture Little Round Top, they were utterly shocked by the sight that awaited them: There, through the smoke and dust near the summit, they caught a glimpse of gleaming bayonet points as a hundred screaming guys from Maine raced down the mountain toward them as fast as they could go.

This was the last straw. Every member of the exhausted Confederate regiment was either killed or captured on the slopes of Little Round Top.

The Union held the line.

On the morning of the third day of the Battle of Gettysburg, Robert E. Lee made the first truly terrible decision of his otherwise impeccable military career. He figured that since the Union was really strong on the hills at the edges of their line, they had to be weak in the center. So he ordered thirteen thousand of his best troops to mass in the middle, form one huge battle line, and try to smash through the soft, meaty underbelly of the Union lines.

Most of the men in this now infamous attack, forever known in military history as Pickett's Charge, knew that this was basically a suicide mission. Veteran soldiers, these men realized they were being asked to march across a mile and a half of wide-open territory, where they'd come under fire from every single gun on the Union line—plus the cannons the Union had installed on Little Round Top and Culp's Hill in the middle of the night—and then assault heavily fortified positions that were defended by a force that outnumbered them.

Still, when the order to attack came, the Army of Northern Virginia formed up into ranks and stepped out of the forest into the open field. With battle flags fluttering in the air and bayonets glinting in the sun, an ocean of gray burst forth in perfect step in an epic, doomed, all-or-nothing march toward the Federal positions. One Union officer would later say, "It was the most beautiful thing I ever saw."

It was a massacre. Hammered by cannonballs, rifle fire, shrapnel bombs, and point-blank canister shots that essentially turned a Civil War cannon into a two-ton shotgun, the Confederates were mowed down by the Federal forces like ducks in a shooting gallery. Entire regiments were wiped out with a single blast from Federal artillery. Wounded and dying men littered the open field. Yet still the Rebels came on.

They reached the wall in only one spot—a bend in the Union lines known as The Angle. Putting his hat on the edge of his sword, Confederate general Lewis Armistead scrambled up onto Cemetery Ridge, leading the remnants of his men charging into the heart of the Federal position. Armistead and his troops managed to overrun the front lines of the Union forces, but

as they were trying to turn the captured Federal guns around on their former owners, the Rebels were counterattacked by regiments from Massachusetts, New York, and Pennsylvania. Armistead's men were killed or captured where they stood.

As the shattered, broken remains of his army limped back toward Confederate lines, Robert E. Lee rode out to meet them. All he could say was "It's all my fault."

Of the thirteen thousand elite veterans who were part of Pickett's Charge, fewer than half made it back. Every regimental commander was dead or wounded on the field. It was such a disaster that Robert E. Lee would submit his resignation to Confederate president Jefferson Davis the following morning. (Davis refused it.)

For all its bravery, Pickett's Charge would be the high-water mark of the Confederacy. Rebel losses on that day were simply too great to replace, and while the war would go on for two more years, the South would never again have the resources or manpower to attempt another attack on Union soil. The tide of the war—and US history—was about to change dramatically.

Age Is Just a Number

When fighting broke out at Gettysburg, a local resident named John L. Burns promptly grabbed his old-school flintlock musket and ran out to the front lines. Burns, a sixty-nine-year-old geezer who had fought in the Mexican-American War and the War of 1812, joined up with the Seventh Wisconsin, fought with the "Iron Brigade" throughout the first day of the battle, and was wounded by three musket balls to various parts of his person. He survived the battle, shook hands with Abraham Lincoln afterward, and then calmly went back to his house.

Survivor

After the war, Joshua Lawrence Chamberlain became the president of Bowdoin College and served as a four-term governor of Maine. During the war he'd survived twenty battles, had six horses shot out from under him, was wounded six times, and was cited four times for bravery. He received the Medal of Honor for his actions on Little Round Top. Chamberlain personally oversaw the surrender of the Confederate infantry at the end of the war, ordering his men to salute in respect as the enemy laid down their weapons.

The Deadliest Brigade

The highest casualty rate of any brigade in the Civil War belongs
to the Federal "Iron Brigade," a unit of Wisconsin and Indiana
troops who were right in the middle of the action at Gettysburg. Known for their distinctive black hats (as opposed to the
typical blue Union kepi hat), the Iron Brigade actually earned
their nickname from Stonewall Jackson, after he saw their grit
firsthand during close-quarters fighting at the Second Bull Run.
The Black Hats lost more than half their men defending Semi-
nary Ridge at Gettysburg.

Joseph H. De Castro

The first Hispanic American to receive the Medal of Honor was
Corporal Joseph H. De Castro, the standard-bearer of the Nineteenth Massachusetts Infantry. During the high-octane fight at
The Angle during Pickett's Charge, De Castro was on the wall
when it was stormed by Garnett's Brigade, and he ran forward
and, only with his regimental flag, battled the standard-bearer
of the Nineteenth Virginia Infantry and captured the enemy's
colors. De Castro rushed back to his commanding general, handed
him the captured banner, then immediately turned around and
headed back into the fray.

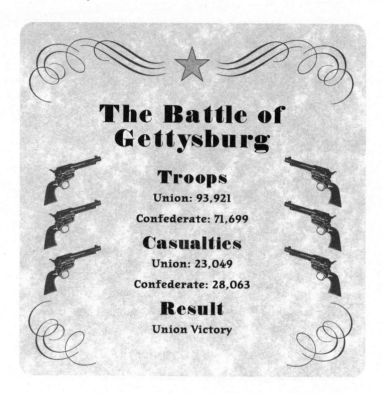

The Battle of Gettysburg

Troops
Union: 93,921

Confederate: 71,699

Casualties
Union: 23,049

Confederate: 28,063

Result
Union Victory

THE GETTYSBURG ADDRESS

As the Union dead were buried on the field at Gettysburg, President Abraham Lincoln gave this eulogy, now known as the Gettysburg Address. It endures throughout history as one of the most famous presidential speeches of all time.

Fourscore and seven years ago our fathers brought forth upon this continent a new nation, conceived in Liberty, and dedicated to the proposition that all men are created equal.

Now we are engaged in a great civil war, testing whether that nation, or any nation so conceived and so dedicated, can long endure. We are met on a great battle-field of that war. We have come to dedicate a portion of that field, as the final resting place of those who here gave their lives that that nation might live. It is altogether fitting and proper that we should do this.

But, in a larger sense, we cannot dedicate, we cannot consecrate, we cannot hallow this ground. The brave men, living and dead, who struggled here, have consecrated it, far above our poor power to add or detract. The world will little note, nor long remember, what we say here, but it can never forget what they did here. It is for us, the living, rather, to be dedicated here to the unfinished work that they who fought here have thus far so nobly advanced. It is rather for us to be here dedicated to the great task remaining before us, that from these honored dead we take increased devotion to that cause for which they here gave the last full measure of devotion; that we here highly resolve that these dead shall not have died in vain; that this nation, under God, shall have a new birth of freedom, and that government of the people, by the people, for the people, shall not perish from the earth.

Vicksburg

One day after the defeat at Gettysburg, the Confederates received more bad news—Vicksburg, Mississippi, the last Confederate stronghold on the Mississippi River, had fallen, her beleaguered defenders finally surrendering after a brilliant months-long siege orchestrated by Union general Ulysses S. Grant. The Mississippi River now belonged to the United States of America. Much-needed Texas beef, new recruits from Arkansas, Louisiana sugar, and the crucial blockade-runner ports at Galveston and New Orleans were completely cut off from supplying the Confederate army.

An imposing hilltop fortress with dozens of gigantic ship-killing guns overlooking the Mississippi, Vicksburg had controlled all traffic on her portion of the country's largest river, and Grant knew that if he wanted to be able to bring up supplies to support an offensive into the Deep South, he needed to capture this Rebel base.

He sent troops to attack nearby towns, cavalry to raid Confederate forces farther inland, and then launched a series of assaults basically everywhere except Vicksburg itself, hoping to get the Rebels to send men to help weaken their position. They did, mostly because they didn't have any other choice if they wanted to keep their supply lines active so they'd, you know, have bullets for their guns and stuff.

Then, while all this was going on, Grant crossed his

entire army over the mighty Mississippi River, marched his men down the far bank, crossed them *back* over the largest river in North America, then hit them from the south, which was, naturally, the last direction Vicksburg expected to be attacked from. Grant walked right up to the gates, surrounded the town, and blocked all Rebel troops and supplies from getting in or out.

The defenders, reduced to eating rats and shoe leather in a squalid fortress devoid of food or medical supplies, held out for two full months before finally surrendering to Grant on July 4, 1863. This defeat, coupled with Gettysburg the day before, would decisively turn the tide of war against the Confederacy.

Federal artillery at Vicksburg

The Making of the Confederate Navy

James D. Bulloch, Raphael Semmes, and the CSS *Alabama*

*Liverpool, England * 1861–1865*

> The eyes of all Europe are at this moment on you. The flag that floats over you is that of a young republic that bids defiance to her enemies, whenever and wherever found. Show the world you know how to uphold it. Go to your quarters.

—Raphael Semmes, captain, CSS *Alabama*

IN APRIL 1861, THEODORE ROOSEVELT'S UNCLE was given a million dollars in gold and a train ticket to Detroit and ordered to turn it into a Confederate navy.

He was told that he should expect to receive no further support, that his work was potentially considered treason by the US government, and that if he were captured and sentenced to death by hanging, the Confederacy would more than likely disavow all knowledge of his existence. Meanwhile, the Atlantic coast was swarming with the watchful eyes of the omnipresent Federal blockading fleet, the Rebels had virtually no warships to speak of whatsoever, no docks or facilities with which to actually build warships, and very little budget for outfitting and equipping them.

James Dunwoody Bulloch cracked his knuckles, waxed his amazing sideburns, and got to work immediately.

Bulloch, a thirty-eight-year-old former US Navy officer turned civilian merchant shipping expert, had offered his services to the Rebellion at the first sign of secession. He grabbed his favorite fake ID, hopped the first train to Detroit, snuck across the border to Canada, bought passage to England on board a Canadian mail steamer, and then proceeded to secretly make contact with every private shipbuilding corporation this side of Stonehenge. Operating as a clandestine cloak-and-dagger Rebel secret agent in Europe, this Georgian used a subtle, delicate mix of deception, diplomacy, and good old-fashioned bribery to grease the wheels of England's dockyards, pretending to be a private shipping contractor so he didn't get torched for violating England's official policy of "supreme neutrality in the war—holy cow,

ow what you're talking about when you
nfederacy, blokes." Bulloch's guile, cun-
ard cash helped him find a few prestigious
agreed to build a series of unarmed "civilian
tra.   .at just so happened to look a *lot* like warships
with no guns on them, and then he somehow managed to
convince the semi-uptight British government to approve
permits for their construction.

When snooping Union agents in London caught wind that
some fishy stuff was going down at the wharf, they raced
over in their fastest horse-drawn carriages to uncover evidence of Bulloch's plan and put an end to it before he flooded
the ocean with enough warships to choke a narwhal. Bulloch,
awesomely labeled by the US government as "the Most Dangerous Man in Europe," continued to elude Federal agents—
he took different routes to work every morning, met with
different contacts at different agencies, and generally just
did everything in his power to throw the Feds off his trail. He
arranged for the construction of dozens of ships, providing
hand-drawn specs to the builders of exactly what he wanted,
and then set up connections so that Rebel transports that
slipped past the Federal blockade could trade their cotton
for British gold. If that wasn't enough, Bulloch also got fake
paperwork for his ships' crews and set up an international
conspiracy with port officials across the world to allow Confederate ships to stop there to resupply and rearm.

Union spies continually tried to stop Bulloch, but since he was operating in Jolly Olde Neutral England, they couldn't put their hands on him without it being a violation of British policy and English Premier League rules—if they wanted to arrest him as a spy or a traitor, they had to have rock-solid evidence on this guy, and Bulloch was like the Al Capone of building Rebel gunboats. When the Union protested his ships, Bulloch argued that there was

nothing illegal about a guy buying private, regular old
ships with twenty-plus weapons-mounting ports that could
maybe someday be built into commerce-killing warships,
and the British Crown agreed with him...mostly because
they really, really wanted that million in gold (depending
on how you want to calculate inflation, one million dollars
in 1864 would be worth about thirteen million in today's
money).

If that's not enough, while the Feds were spending all
their energy trying to nail Bulloch on his warship program,
this guy snuck out a back door, purchased thirteen thousand Enfield rifles, supplies, and ammunition in Scotland,
personally sailed them to the Azores on a British-flagged
ship, eluded US Customs agents in Bermuda, ran the Federal blockade, and dropped off his gear in Savannah before
heading back to England on a different ship. It would be
the biggest haul of weaponry ever smuggled in by a Confederate blockade runner, and, as a cherry on top, the ship
Bulloch brought over was refitted as an ironclad warship.
And that was just like a fun weekend trip for this guy.

During his career as a Rebel secret agent in London,
Bulloch successfully oversaw the construction of forty-nine
blockade runners and commerce raiders that would oper-
ate in ports ranging from France to Brazil to Australia.
He financed a network of covert agents, collected intel on
US naval movements, and oversaw a lethal surface fleet that

sank 130 Union vessels ranging from warships to whaling vessels and merchant traders.

The most famous of these daring commerce raiders was the second one he constructed—a sleek, 230-foot wooden ship initially known only by the code name "Number 290."

Number 290 was a beauty. She had a full set of sails and old-school pirate ship–style rigging, but if it needed to make extra speed she could also drop a pair of three-hundred-horsepower steam-powered propellers into the water and haul outta there at blazing speeds that left other boats eating her ocean spray. It had mounting ports for enough weapons to scare commerce and do battle with warships, a device that turned ocean vapors into drinkable water, and a reinforced hull that could absorb some serious punishment. When Union spies snuck into the Liverpool dockyards and saw this baby sitting there looking awesome, they frantically demanded British authorities impound the vessel immediately. The Brits signed the order the following morning and ordered Number 290 grounded pending investigation.

Except by the time the Royal agents arrived with the paperwork to impound the ship, it was already gone. Bulloch had been tipped off, personally bolted on board, ran it past the USS *Tuscarora* in the English Channel, reached the North Atlantic, raised the Confederate flag, and rechristened Number 290 the CSS *Alabama*.

Bulloch thought the *Alabama* was so baller that he

wanted to captain it himself, but he was too valuable as a secret agent, so command of the *Alabama* was handed over to a Marylander named Raphael Semmes instead. Semmes, an orphan turned lawyer with thirty-five years of naval warfare experience, had already captured eighteen Union merchant ships while commanding the rickety old wooden boat CSS *Sumter* in the early days of the war. Semmes was dashing and brave, had a sweet *Three Musketeers*–style waxed 'stache, and now he was commanding a raiding vessel that was twice the ship *Sumter* ever was.

Outfitted with eight cannons, led by twenty-four Confederate officers (including Bulloch's half brother Irvine), and crewed by 120 Spanish, British, Dutch, and Irish mercenaries, the CSS *Alabama* went nuts on American merchant shipping, seeking not to destroy the US Navy but to inflict so much destruction on US commerce that it would cripple the American economy so hard they'd have to dig through the couch cushions for spare change every time they wanted to buy a rifle.

Semmes's first targets were New England whaling ships operating out of the Azores islands near Europe. His strategy was to approach an unarmed commercial ship at high speed, board it pirate-style, plunder every single bit of gold, coal, food, wine, cash, and weaponry on board, then drop the crew on an island somewhere and burn the ship. For all intents and purposes, the CSS *Alabama* carried out state-sponsored piracy in the coolest way possible, and Raphael Semmes was the swashbuckling Jack Sparrow dude plundering and pillaging every US-flagged vessel from London to Boston.

After slapping around whaling ships in the North Atlantic, Semmes moved closer to the States, preying primarily on New England food and grain shipping. Basically, the pipeline worked like this—corn, grain, and other delicious foods would be harvested in the Midwest, sent to New York by rail, then to Europe by sea, where it was traded for gold that was then sent back to New York and turned into bullets and payroll for the US Army. If the Confederate army needed food, Semmes hit the ships on their way to Europe. If the Rebel government needed money, Semmes hit the ships on their way back. It was like taking candy from a three-hundred-foot-long wooden baby that floats on water.

Naturally, it didn't take long for a guy like Semmes to develop a reputation for being a stone-cold sea-pillager. In the South, he was a romantic Robin Hood–style hero, robbing the corrupt Union to aid the cause. To the New York media, he was a notorious, bloodthirsty pirate with terrible hygiene who single-handedly drove marine insurance rates up by a factor of six. I'd argue both descriptions are equally awesome.

Soon the US Navy got off their butts and sent ships to hunt these nautical raiders down, but Semmes consistently eluded them, including one time when he avoided capture by taking his ship through the center of a hurricane in the Caribbean just to prove that they shouldn't try to mess with a dude who surfs monsoons. His most daring escape, however, came in Venezuela, when Semmes was tracked down and cornered in the harbor by a huge US warship. The American vessel couldn't attack Semmes in a neutral harbor, so it parked in international waters and just waited for him to come out so they could blast him into driftwood. The towering US ship spent all day gearing up for battle in full view of the *Alabama*. Semmes ordered his men to rig for battle and prepare to fight, then sent a letter to the American ship telling them how he was going to beat them silly first thing the next morning.

But when the sun came up, Semmes was gone. The CSS *Alabama* had gone dark and slipped out in the middle of the night.

Semmes's mission was to plunder, not fight battles, but that doesn't mean he didn't get into a scrape or two during his travels. One time, off the coast of Galveston, Texas, the *Alabama* randomly ran into the Union warship USS *Hatteras* in the middle of the night. The *Hatteras*, not recognizing the *Alabama*, ordered Semmes to identify himself, so Semmes sailed right up next to the *Hatteras*, raised the Rebel flag, and pasted the *Hatteras* with an eight-gun salute. The two warships charged toward each other, the ill-tempered crews shooting at one another with muskets from the deck, and after a short, intense firefight, the *Alabama* set her nemesis on fire, aerated her engine with a cannonball, and forced the *Hatteras*'s surrender. It would be the only time a Confederate ship would sink a Union warship on the high seas. Semmes pulled the crew of the *Hatteras* out of the ocean, dropped them off at Jamaica (not a bad place to be marooned), and went back to work.

For the next twenty-two months, Semmes and the *Alabama*, operating without a home base, sailed through Cuba, the Caribbean, Brazil, and South Africa, rounding the Cape of Good Hope before going to India and Singapore and resupplying with agents arranged by James Bulloch back in Liverpool. By now Bulloch was running an empire that had brought Union shipping to its knees. Everywhere the *Alabama* put into port, she was greeted by flocks of people eager to catch a glimpse of the American Civil War firsthand, and every time she left, you could pretty much count on a Union warship or two showing up a few days later.

As is the case with most pirates and sea-raiders, the *Alabama*'s luck eventually ran out, and while she was put into port in Cherbourg, France, for a badly needed refit, the *Alabama* was blocked in by the USS *Kearsarge*—a bigger, better-armed, armored Federal warship commanded by Captain John A. Winslow, a North Carolina–born abolitionist and Raphael Semmes's former roommate aboard the USS *Raritan* during the Mexican-American War.

Semmes didn't flinch. He sent a letter to his old buddy saying, "My intention is to fight the *Kearsarge* as soon as I can make the necessary arrangements. I hope these will not detain me more than until tomorrow evening or after the morrow morning at the furthest. I beg she will not depart before I am ready to depart."

Translation: Stay right there. I'm coming to get you.

Knowing this would probably be his last fight, Semmes left all of his captured gold and gear ashore with Confederate agents and set sail out of Cherbourg Harbor at ten AM on June 19, 1864, leaving behind a port with fifteen thousand French citizens crowded shoulder to shoulder and lined up on the rooftops to watch the impending showdown.

The battle lasted a little over an hour, both warships maneuvering around and nailing each other with every gun they had. Semmes fought his ship well, but the eleven-inch Dahlgren guns of the *Kearsarge* were too much for the battered, worn-out *Alabama* to handle, and after several volleys the much-feared Rebel sea-raider caught fire and began sinking. Semmes ordered the abandon ship, threw his sword into the ocean, and jumped overboard as the *Alabama* sank beneath the waves. It wouldn't be seen again until a French expedition located it in 1984.

Most of the crew of the *Alabama* were picked up by the *Kearsarge* and taken as prisoners of war, but one British yacht named the *Deerhound* came flying in out of nowhere

and pulled up forty-two Confederate survivors, including Captain Semmes himself, who was taken back to England to continue the fight. Captain Winslow, meanwhile, would be rewarded for destroying the *Alabama* with a twenty-five-thousand-dollar check from the New York City Chamber of Commerce—no small chunk of change, especially in 1864, when a dollar was about the equivalent of eleven bucks today.

In nearly two years at sea, Semmes and the *Alabama* sailed seventy-five thousand miles across three oceans, attacking merchant ships, trading vessels, whaling boats, warships, and pretty much anything on the ocean that was sailing underneath the Stars and Stripes. During her raiding career, the *Alabama* sank, captured, burned, or otherwise mutilated sixty-nine Union-flagged vessels, dealing over $6.5 million in damage to the American economy. After the war Semmes would be brought up on charges of piracy, but judges dismissed the case, probably on account of Semmes not having either an eye patch or a peg leg.

The United States did, however, have a decent case for England violating its neutrality by building a warship for the Confederacy, and after the war a court mandated that the UK pay the States $15.5 million in reparations for the destruction caused by Bulloch's fleet of commerce raiders. The *Alabama* accounted for nearly half of the destruction.

As for Bulloch, near the end of the war he attempted to

organize a plot to kidnap and assassinate Lincoln, but he never carried it out. He spent the rest of his life in exile in England, refusing to repatriate as an American citizen. His family didn't seem to have the same problem—Bulloch's nephew Teddy Roosevelt would be a future president, and his grandniece, Eleanor Roosevelt, would be the country's first lady alongside President Franklin Delano Roosevelt during World War II.

The Last Flag

The last Confederate flag was lowered on November 6, 1865, by Lieutenant Commander James Waddell of the CSS *Shenandoah*, an eight-gun, 230-foot auxiliary screw steamship commissioned by Bulloch to similar specs as the *Alabama*. Operating out of a base in Australia, the *Shenandoah* captured or destroyed thirty-eight US-flagged whaling ships in the South Pacific, causing an estimated $1.36 million in damages to the Federal economy. Waddell didn't hear the war was over until a British whaling ship informed him in August 1865 (well after the war was over), so he took the seventy-three-man crew to England (becoming the only Rebel ship to circle the globe in the process) and surrendered the vessel to the British. The Brits then resold it to the sultan of Zanzibar, who accidentally sank it.

CSS *Alabama* Versus USS *Hatteras*

Sailors

Union: 126

Confederate: 145

Casualties

Union: 7, plus 118 captured

Confederate: 2

Result

Confederate Victory

CSS *Alabama* sinks USS *Hatteras*, January 1863

The Fifty-Fourth Massachusetts

The Assault on Fort Wagner

*Morris Island, South Carolina * July 18, 1863*

Never since the world began was a better chance offered to a long enslaved and oppressed people. The opportunity is given us to be men. With one courageous resolution we may blot out the hand-writing of ages against us. Once let the black man get upon his person the brass letters *U.S.*, let him get an eagle on his button, and a musket on his shoulder, and bullets in his pocket, and there is no power on earth or under the earth which can deny that he has earned the right of citizenship in the United States. I say again, this is our chance, and woe betide us if we fail to embrace it.

—Frederick Douglass, antislavery activist and former slave

ON JANUARY 1, 1863, PRESIDENT ABRAHAM
Lincoln used his power not as chief executive but as the
commander in chief of the US Army to issue the Emancipation
Proclamation—a document formally declaring that all slaves
in areas of open rebellion were now going to be treated as free
men by Union troops and by the US government.

Even with the hopefully obvious part about slavery being
one of the most horrible things ever and needing to be purged
from American culture forever, the Emancipation Proclamation was also a truly brilliant tactical move for two reasons:
First, it fundamentally altered the aims of the war for both
sides. Before the proclamation, the majority of Lincoln's rhet-
oric about the war had been about preserving the Union and
keeping the country together; once he laid down this doc,
he was officially saying this was a war about destroying the
institution of slavery, thereby making it *much* less likely that
antislavery European countries like England, Russia, and
France would jump into the war on the side of the Rebels.
Second, making freed slaves eligible to serve in the Union
army as soon as they were freed meant that as the Northern
armies pushed their way through the South, they were able
to immediately replace their dead troops with new recruits
who were ready to seek some good old-fashioned vengeance
on their former overseers and masters.

Of course, there were also plenty of free black men up north
who were more than happy to drop whatever they were doing

and rush to the recruiting office, and just a month after the issuing of the proclamation, the governor of Massachusetts had already organized one of the first African-American regiments to be officially recognized by the Union army—the Fifty-Fourth Massachusetts Volunteer Infantry Regiment. Six hundred fifty men, mostly free blacks from Massachusetts, Ohio, and Pennsylvania, as well as escaped slaves who had made their way north, all banded together to take up arms and fight a war that meant just as much to them as it did to anyone else involved in the conflict.

Now, it's important to note here that not everybody in the North was exactly thrilled by the creation of an all-black regiment. Plenty of uptight white guys were convinced that blacks had "neither the courage nor intelligence" to fight, and one of the deals with the Fifty-Fourth was that while all the enlisted men were black, every officer from the rank of lieutenant up had to be white. Black soldiers were paid less, given crappy menial-labor jobs, put at the bottom of the supply chain for uniforms and weapons, and generally just treated like they didn't know the difference between a bayonet and a loaf of bread, mostly because a large percentage of the white American military command was certain they lacked the will, ability, or intensity to fight as hard as their white counterparts.

The Fifty-Fourth was about to prove them wrong.

Led by twenty-five-year-old Colonel Robert Gould Shaw, a Harvard-educated, über-wealthy Bostonian who had charged the cornfield with the Second Massachusetts Infantry at Antietam, the Fifty-Fourth assembled in parade formation and marched to their troop transports in 1863. They were cheered on by the largest crowd that had ever been assembled in Boston up until this point. After sailing down the coast, the Fifty-Fourth arrived deep in enemy territory, unloading at Hilton Head, South Carolina, on June 3, 1863.

The Fifty-Fourth was assigned to take part in an attempt to capture the port city of Charleston, South Carolina—the first city to secede from the Union, the birthplace of the Confederacy, and a place that was about as intense a Rebel stronghold as anywhere else in the South. Capturing Charleston was a tall order, but successfully taking it would deal the Confederacy a humiliating defeat and also be kind of awesome.

Previous direct assaults on Charleston had been wiped out by intense cannon and rifle fire from the city's fanatical defenders. So by the summer of 1863, the Yankees were trying a new tactic: They were going to take all the little forts and islands in Charleston Harbor, then bombard the city and attack it from the sea with its overwhelming navy. It was here that the men of the Fifty-Fourth would make a name for themselves that would resonate throughout history.

Not long after landing at James Island and capturing a place appropriately named Secessionville, the Fifty-Fourth spilled their first blood of the war in a pretty spectacular fashion on July 16, 1863, when they were assigned to defend one of the island's causeways from an intense Rebel attempt to gobsmack the Union assault and throw them off the island. Three companies (about three hundred men) of the Fifty-Fourth were positioned in defensive entrenchments, bayonets fixed, hoping to rely on their admittedly short training while a larger, more experienced, incredibly terrifying Confederate onslaught came charging out of the woods in their direction, guns blazing. Holding their ground, firing and loading their muskets for all they were worth, the Fifty-Fourth laid down a molten field of lead death, cutting through the Southerners with a swirling mass of vicious gunfire. With a spine-chilling Rebel yell, the Confederate forces reached the Fifty-Fourth's earthworks, bayonets and knives at the ready, and vaulted into the Union trenches.

The Fifty-Fourth made them wish they hadn't.

Swinging rifles like baseball bats, stabbing with bayonets, and gnashing their teeth, the Fifty-Fourth fought with everything from haymaker punches to point-blank musket blasts, battling the Confederates in fierce hand-to-hand combat. The regiment suffered forty-two men killed or wounded in the action, but through their determination they somehow managed to stop the assault and send the Rebels fleeing back across the causeway.

Later that same month the Fifty-Fourth was redeployed to Morris Island to participate in the siege of Fort Wagner—a powerful Confederate position that played a critical role in the defensive ring around Charleston. The Union knew that in order to move on Charleston, they were going to need to attack, capture, and hold this position at all costs.

Colonel Robert Gould Shaw volunteered the Fifty-Fourth Massachusetts to lead the charge.

The Fifty-Fourth, veterans of exactly one battle in their history, had never attacked a fort before, and this really wasn't a great place to start. An imposing fortress manned by dedicated warriors, Fort Wagner had already survived two full Yankee assaults and a couple dozen naval artillery bombardments virtually unscathed—a recent attempt on the outpost left 340 Union troops dead or dying while the defenders only suffered twelve casualties.

For starters, the fort was on a part of the island completely surrounded by impassable swamps, and the only viable approach was along an eighty-foot-wide strip of sand, which is not the ideal thing to be running across while dudes shoot bullets at you. If the attackers somehow miraculously made it across the sand without being cut to pieces by the twenty cannons and 1,700 men defending the fort (not to mention the cannons positioned on Fort Sumter just a mile away, which could easily bombard Union troops as they attacked Wagner), they then had to cross a waist-deep moat, make their way through two eight-hundred-foot-long walls made of sand and wood, then assault the bombproof shelters inside. To make matters worse, the commanding officer of the fort, General William B. Taliaferro (a Virginian who, incidentally, was also Harvard-educated) was under orders by the government of South Carolina to enslave all black prisoners of war and execute any white officer commanding an all-black unit.

Nevertheless, at dusk on July 18, 1863, Colonel Shaw and the six hundred men of the Fifty-Fourth Massachusetts Volunteer Infantry Regiment formed up in battle lines at the head of the Union column. They would lead the charge, followed by several white regiments. Their primary objective was to breach the walls and hold them until reinforcements arrived.

On the shoulders of every man in the unit was the responsibility and duty to prove the value of black soldiers in combat. They weren't fighting just for themselves or for their country, but for their entire race.

Cannon fire erupted down the line as Fort Wagner's guns opened up on them, churning up clouds of sand and dust as the Fifty-Fourth began their assault down that long, narrow, death-filled corridor leading to the imposing walls of the Confederate position. Clouds of smoke belched forth from Confederate musketry as the Federal troops hustled through the difficult, uneven terrain of this uninviting beach, the air alive with the crack of rifle fire and the screams of dying men. Less than a mile off the coast, the Rebel artillery crews at Fort Sumter went to work as well, hurling shells and shrapnel

bombs a half mile across Charleston Harbor into the mass of men rushing for Fort Wagner.

With bayonets fixed on the ends of their Springfield Model 1861 muskets, assault troops from the Fifty-Fourth made their way through the moat, scrambling up the far end and rushing toward the first wood-and-sand wall. Ignoring the crippling fire of Rebel muskets, the Fifty-Fourth climbed toward the wall, coming face-to-face with the first line of Confederate defenders, who by now were falling back toward a second wall farther inside the fort. Swinging their rifles like baseball bats and jamming their bayonets into any man they could reach, the Fifty-Fourth clawed their way up, fighting like warriors the entire way.

The commanding officer was one of the first men atop the wall. Shaw, pulling his sword and screaming for his men to rally behind him, turned to meet the enemy just as a Rebel bullet pierced his heart, killing him instantly. Despite the loss of his commanding officer, Sergeant John Wall, the man tasked with carrying the unit's colors, scrambled and planted the regimental flag—the ultimate symbol of the Fifty-Fourth—into the top of the wall as a beacon to the Union forces that the men from Massachusetts had reached their objective. No sooner had he done this, however, than a bullet ripped into him as well, dropping the flag bearer to his knees with a grievous wound. Before the flag hit the ground, however, it was grabbed by Sergeant William H. Carney, a twenty-three-year-old former slave from Virginia who had escaped through the Underground Railroad, made a life for himself in Boston, and eventually became successful enough to buy his parents out of slavery. Carney, waving the flag for all he was worth and urging his men forward, made an excellent target for Rebel marksmen, but even though he was shot once and received a shrapnel wound from an enemy artillery shell, Carney continued to wave the flag and shout for his boys to get up and over the wall.

The Fifty-Fourth followed, dashing over the wall, but killer fire from the Confederate positions had taken a toll on the men from Massachusetts. The Fifty-Fourth, reinforced by a couple of other regiments, hurled themselves into the fray, fighting with bayonets and muskets and taking Confederate canister fire at point-blank range, but the defenders of the fort battled their guts out, launched a counterattack, and somehow managed to hold their position. By the time the order was issued to fall back, an hour of intense close-quarters combat had taken its toll— of the 5,300 Union troops who assaulted Wagner, 1,515 of them lay dead or dying.

The Fifty-Fourth, the unit that volunteered to lead the charge, lost their commander, two-thirds of their officers, and almost half of their men to Rebel fire, but they had proven their worth as front-line warriors who were more than capable of holding their own against any military force this planet had to offer. Never was this more obvious than in the case of Sergeant Carney, a man who, despite two gushing wounds, resolutely held the flag on the parapet of Fort Wagner for the entire battle. As the Union forces withdrew, Carney limped back with them, holding the flag high even though a third bullet hit him as he was retreating. Carney, half crawling across the bloodstained beach, refused to hand the flag off to any man who offered to help him, saying that he could only trust it to an officer of the Fifty-Fourth. He made it all the way back to Union lines, carrying his unit's banner into the field hospital, where he passed it to a lieutenant in the Fifty-Fourth before collapsing into a bed. The last thing he said before he passed out from loss of blood was, "Boys, the old flag never touched the ground!"

He received a resounding cheer from his comrades.

The Fifty-Fourth, badly undermanned but not yet ready to throw in the towel, replenished their numbers and held the siege of the fort for the next two months. When the Rebels finally abandoned the position in September, the Fifty-Fourth was given the honor of being the first unit to march into the captured enemy stronghold. As a parting gift to Fort Wagner, the Fifty-Fourth repositioned all the guns in the fort to point at downtown Charleston before they shipped out once again, took part in the capture of Jacksonville, Florida, and performed admirably in the largest Civil War engagement in Florida, the Battle of Olustee, on February 20, 1864.

Sergeant Carney would survive the war, marry a schoolteacher, deliver mail for thirty-two years, and live to be sixty-eight. For his actions at Fort Wagner, he would become the first black man in American history to earn the Medal of Honor.

Follow the Flags

Each regiment of the Civil War carried three flags—the national flag, a state or brigade flag, plus a special flag created specifically for their regiment. Typically hand-stitched for the regiment by the women of their hometown and presented to the unit before they departed for war, these flags served not only to boost morale, reminding the men of their heritage and their homes, but also to show the unit where it needed to be—the flags were usually to the front and right of the formation, so if you got lost during the fight, you could look up and try to make sure you were between the flags. As units would progress through the war, they would add names of battles and engagements to it, and they would not repair battle damage done to the flag by bullets or shrapnel. There was no greater honor than to be the man carrying the flag, no greater glory than to capture an enemy flag, and no greater humiliation than to have your regiment's flag fall into enemy hands.

Robert Blake

While William Carney was the first black man to earn a Medal of Honor, the first one to physically receive the medal was Robert Blake, an escaped South Carolina slave working as a ship's gunner aboard the USS *Marblehead*. When a Confederate shore gun hit his ship, blasting apart a gun crew, Blake braved intense fire to run powder back and forth to the still-functioning guns, oblivious to the danger around him. All told, twenty-five African Americans would receive Medals of Honor for actions during the Civil War.

Frederick Douglass

Born into slavery in Maryland, Frederick Douglass taught himself how to read and write, escaped to Massachusetts, became a bestselling author and vocal abolitionist, and ended up founding and editing a couple newspapers and political journals, like the popular abolitionist weekly newsletter *The North Star*. One of the first black civil rights leaders, Douglass championed abolition, voting rights, and citizenship for the African-American community, and urged black men to enlist in the Union army. Both of his sons served in the Fifty-Fourth Massachusetts.

The Thirteenth Amendment

It's important to note that the Emancipation Proclamation only freed the slaves in areas of open rebellion, and that it remained legal to own slaves in the border states. It wasn't until the Thirteenth Amendment, passed through Congress in February 1865 and ratified in December 1865, that slavery was abolished officially across the United States.

Roughly 179,000 black men served as soldiers in the US Army, making up about 10 percent of their enlistment, and another nineteen thousand served in the navy. Nearly forty thousand black troops died over the course of the war, almost thirty thousand of them from disease or illness.

The Battle of Fort Wagner

Troops
Union: 5,000

Confederate: 1,800

Casualties
Union: 1,515

Confederate: 174

Result
Union Victory

Harriet Tubman

There was one of two things I had a right to— liberty, or death. If I could not have one I would have the other; for no man should take me alive.

—Harriet Tubman

The Underground Railroad is well known for having transported thousands of slaves to freedom both before and during the Civil War, but the term *railroad* really makes the whole thing sound a heck of a lot less dangerous and life-threatening than it actually was. We're not talking about a relaxing ride on the subway here, folks. This was perilous undercover travel deep behind enemy lines, where the slightest misstep could result in the destruction of the entire Railroad system and capture meant a lifetime of savage beatings and humiliating, backbreaking servitude. This wasn't an enterprise taken up by spineless weaklings, a fact that was never better illustrated than by the unbelievable story of Harriet Tubman.

Born into slavery on a Maryland plantation, Harriet spent her first twenty-five years living under the watchful gaze of a number of different overseers and housemistresses. While this five-foot-tall woman may not have been the most physically imposing specimen, hard work made her tough—she toned her muscles by doing grueling manual labor twelve hours a day, seven days a

week, chopping firewood and plowing fields in the unfor-
giving sun.

Despite facing a lifetime of bondage, Harriet Tubman
never backed down from anybody. Her stubbornness generally resulted in her suffering endless beatings and physical
abuse, including once when she was smashed in the head
with a lead weight for defending a fellow slave (a wound
that left her suffering dizzy spells and light-headedness
for the rest of her life). But she simply refused to have her
spirit broken by a bunch of jerks on a power trip. Finally,
one cloudy night in 1849, Harriet Tubman had had enough.
She made a break for freedom. Fleeing into the darkness,
Tubman traveled for several days through the unfamiliar
Maryland wilderness and didn't look back until she reached
the friendly, "we promise we won't enslave you" confines of
Philadelphia.

As awesome as it was to no longer live in slavery, there
was still one problem—Harriet left behind her mother,
father, and nine siblings. While most people would have just
shrugged and said, "Forget it, dudes, you're on your own,"
Harriet Tubman did the unbelievable—she went *back* to
the plantation, tracked down her family, and led *them* to
freedom.

Once Harriet saw that she was capable of leading a large
band of fugitive slaves safely through hostile territory,
she decided that she couldn't enjoy her freedom while her
people remained in bondage. Using the code name Moses,
she returned to Maryland *twenty* more times, each time

delivering people from the chains of slavery to the promised land (which in this case was Niagara Falls, Canada, a 350-mile walk from the Maryland border), where they didn't have to worry about things like getting whipped for insubordination or not having enough food to eat. Tubman rescued more than three hundred slaves over the course of twenty years and was one of the greatest and most fearless heroines of antebellum America.

Deep behind enemy lines for days and weeks at a time, Tubman and her crew slept in swamps, hid during the day,

and moved under the cover of darkness. Traveling with women and children, young and old, and being pursued relentlessly by police, soldiers, attack dogs, bounty hunters, and slave-catchers barely caused her to flinch. She urged her people on, not only by leading with her iron will but also by threatening to shoot anybody who suggested giving up or turning back. (Seriously, if one member was caught or returned, it jeopardized the entire Railroad, and she would rather have killed a person than seen that go down. Luckily, it never came to that.) Although she was illiterate and uneducated, Harriet Tubman was by no means stupid. She cleverly hid from her would-be captors, lived off the land, and made her escapes on Saturdays, which bought her a one-day head start because wanted posters could not legally be posted on Sundays—twenty-four hours was all she needed to leave her enemies in her dust. Despite the fact that there was a forty-thousand-dollar reward (a figure that today equates to a cool four mil) for the "black ghost," she was never caught and never lost a single person she escorted to freedom.

When Tubman wasn't risking her life trying to save people from bondage, she spoke out publicly against slavery, worked at a hotel, and helped John Brown plan and finance his attack on the federal arsenal at Harper's Ferry, West Virginia. When the Civil War blew up, she signed on as a scout with the Union army, serving as a reconnaissance officer for Colonel James Montgomery. As a scout and spy, Tubman helped slaves escape the South, provided them with medical attention, and encouraged them to enlist in the Federal army. She also participated in a number of military engagements, including the Raid at Combahee Ferry in 1863, when she personally helped liberate eight hundred slaves in a single battle. Amazingly, she wasn't even paid for her work, instead earning her money by brewing barrels of presumably delicious homemade root beer for the soldiers.

In the 1890s, Tubman had brain surgery, without anesthesia. She allegedly bit down on a bullet for the pain. Is that tough enough for you?

After the war she received a military pension, built a house in upstate New York, and opened up a rest/retirement home for elderly black men and women. Even into her later years she stood up for her rights, fighting for women's suf-

frage alongside cool ladies like Susan B. Anthony and Emily Howland. She died in 1913 at the age of ninety-three and was buried with full military honors.

Harriet Tubman, probably at her home in Auburn, New York, 1911

Morgan's Raid

The Great Raid of 1863

Kentucky, Indiana, and Ohio ✶ June 18–July 26, 1863

> In no other way does the enemy give us so much trouble, at so little expense to himself, as by the raids of rapidly moving small bodies of troops...harassing, and discouraging loyal residents, supplying themselves with provisions, clothing, horses, and the like, surprising and capturing small detachments of our forces, and breaking our communications.
>
> —President Abraham Lincoln

AT NINE O'CLOCK ON THE MORNING OF July 10, 1863, the citizens of the quiet town of Salem, Indiana, were drawn out of their homes by a sound that was highly unfamiliar to this part of the United States—the sound of gunfire, shouting, and the trampling hooves of thousands of horsemen charging hard in their direction.

John Hunt Morgan was coming.

The defenders of Salem, a few hundred brave and dedicated but highly inexperienced men from the Indiana Legion, a "break glass in case of emergency" militia force that had never seen combat before, grabbed their rifles and sprinted down Salem's dirt roads toward the action. The men drew themselves into a hasty defensive position around the outskirts of town and loaded their muskets, sighting down their shaking barrels at the woods before them, awaiting orders from their probably-freaked-out commanding officer.

They were not at all prepared to deal with 1,500 battle-hardened, handpicked Confederate raiders charging out of the woods on horseback at a full gallop, the bearded, grizzled veterans firing six-shooters and carbines in all directions, cutting down everything in their path.

Things like this weren't supposed to happen in Indiana. Not when the rest of the Civil War was taking place about a thousand miles south, down in Tennessee and Mississippi. Not when the Union was supposed to be winning, and the Rebels were supposed to be on the run.

The legion, facing a superior cavalry force equipped with rapid-firing pistols, ridiculously bad attitudes, and the occasional razor-sharp cavalry saber, broke and ran for it or died where they stood. The Confederate raiders swarmed through the town, burned the railroad station, torched train cars, blew up both bridges, ransacked stores for supplies, and

forced the town's flour mills to pay thousand-dollar ransoms (an exorbitant expense in Civil War days) to avoid having their places of business demolished. By noon they'd already hauled out of there with everything from ammunition boxes to expensive chafing dishes hanging from their saddles, the nineteenth-century version of Vikings raiding, pillaging, and then fading away before reinforcements could arrive.

At the head of this force of raiders was thirty-eight-year-old Brigadier General John Hunt Morgan, a dashing horseman with an excellent mustache who rode tall in the saddle, never backing away from a fight. He was a man so well known for striking hard, stopping only to plunder, burn, and receive kisses from Southern belles, that his nickname in the Rebel papers was "the Confederate Thunderbolt."

Morgan was born in Huntsville, Alabama, but spent most of his life living with his aristocratic family in Lexington, Kentucky. He'd enlisted in the US Army after being suspended from Transylvania University for dueling with a classmate, fought with distinction in the Mexican-American War, and then retired and owned a hemp factory in Lexington. When the Civil War broke out, Kentucky tried to remain neutral, not wanting to secede but also refusing to raise arms against the South. John Hunt Morgan had no such hang-ups. When the Union confiscated his factory, Morgan raised a militia of horsemen, headed south, and mustered them in as the Second Kentucky Cavalry. He spent the early years of the war as a scout and reconnaissance trooper and commanded his regiment at the Battle of Shiloh, but he quickly realized that hit-and-run raids behind enemy lines were his personal specialty and started volunteering for the most dangerous missions he could possibly undertake.

Morgan's first raid took place in July and August 1862. He was ordered to head behind Union lines to cause chaos and disrupt an attempt by the Federals to capture Chattanooga, so Morgan rode eight hundred men around enemy lines, burned a couple of steamboats, severed General Don Carlos Buell's communication lines with Louisville, traveled one thousand miles, captured twelve hundred prisoners, lost just one hundred men, and severely messed up the Federals' mojo. Two months later, Morgan went on another raid through Federal lines, destroying railroad stations, communication lines, bridges, and supply depots. He captured the town of Hartsville, Tennessee, then printed a newspaper on a stolen printing press to distribute to Southern citizens, letting them know that Morgan was there and that he was pretty friggin' awesome. As if that wasn't enough, Morgan then went on a third raid just two months later, destroying the railroad line at Munfordville on Christmas Eve, capturing the town of Rolling Fork, and ruining two million dollars' worth of Union supplies. He somehow got his entire command back to Rebel lines despite having half the Union army chasing him down, and then married the daughter of his commanding officer

when he got home. The Union branded him a dangerous outlaw, but in nearly every one of the Kentucky and Tennessee
towns he rode into, citizens would come running out of their
homes to give him flowers and bacon and candy, which was
probably pretty great for him.

This raid, Morgan's fourth in the last calendar year, was
different. He'd been sent to stall the Union's newest attempt
to capture Chattanooga, and ordered to limit his operations
to Kentucky and Tennessee, but when John Hunt Morgan led
about 2,500 hand-selected horsemen and four horse-drawn
cannons out of Sparta, Tennessee, on June 18, 1863, he had
other ideas.

Morgan had no intention of stopping at the Kentucky border. He was going to take the fight to the Federals, ride Confederate troops into Indiana, Ohio, and Pennsylvania, and
then hook up with Robert E. Lee just in time to participate in
the Battle of Gettysburg.

With only local militia directly opposing him, Morgan
burned a trail through Union supply lines in Tennessee and
Kentucky, then turned north, captured two Union steamboats, and crossed the Ohio River into Indiana. He seized the
towns of Corydon and Salem, scared half the population of
Cincinnati into fleeing their homes, and stole two thousand
hams from the town of Dupont because I guess these guys
just really loved ham or something.

Like his previous raids, John Hunt Morgan's mission was

to cause as much chaos and anarchy as possible, lighting up every flammable thing he could find, leading Union troops around in circles, and preventing the Federals from bringing supplies and reinforcements to the front lines. He'd charge into battle when the opportunity presented itself, but most times he used cunning and ingenuity to keep as many of his men alive as possible.

His favorite tactic was to dress in stolen Federal uniforms, wait in the middle of the road, and stop wagon trains of enemy supplies, pretending he was a Union officer checking passes. As soon as Morgan and his men would get close, they'd draw their pistols, take the Federal soldiers' weapons, plunder the wagons, and escape into the night. Another popular tactic was to seize a telegraph office, chase out the telegraph operator, steal his codebooks and secret dispatches, and then send fake orders to get enemy troops to move away from wherever Morgan was headed. One time he captured a

train Jesse James–style and found it completely packed full of Union troops, so he disarmed the enemy soldiers, stole eight thousand dollars in cash from the passengers, and then invited the Yankee officers and their wives to have lunch with him and his men. They did, and after lunch was over, Morgan opted not to burn the train because he didn't want to make such nice ladies walk all the way to the next town.

But it wasn't all fun and games for John Hunt Morgan and his crew of merry men. Hot on their heels was another Kentucky boy, Brigadier General Edward Hobson, a loyal Union soldier who was riding fast at the head of ten thousand Federal cavalry seeking to put an end to this madness. Hobson followed the trail of this gunslinging *Where's Waldo*, chasing Morgan from town to town, constantly closing the net around this dangerous outlaw who was annoyingly burning all these towns and railroad stations and messing up the North's attempts to reunite the country under one flag.

Hobson caught up with Morgan in Ohio, forcing the Confederate raider to ride ninety miles in just thirty-six hours to escape being completely surrounded. Pressed by Hobson, Morgan raced for the Pennsylvania border, hoping to meet up with Lee's forces. But when he reached the Ohio River, Morgan was shocked to see Hobson waiting for him with fourteen thousand men and a half-dozen Union gunboats parked in the middle of the river. The ensuing battle left 120 of Morgan's men killed and seven hundred captured, but Morgan, ever a survivor, escaped with three hundred men and kept running for it. He eluded Hobson for another week, finally surrendering on July 26, in the sweltering heat just ninety miles south of Lake Erie. It would be the farthest north any uniformed Confederate soldier would ever reach.

In his forty-six-day raid, John Hunt Morgan rode over one thousand miles, captured six thousand prisoners, destroyed twenty-five bridges, demolished hundreds of miles of railroad lines, stole two thousand horses, and ransacked millions of dollars' worth of loot from businesses and supply depots. Despite his being a commissioned Confederate officer, the Union was really, really unhappy about all this raiding nonsense, so they convicted Morgan of being an outlaw and a horse thief and sentenced him to twenty years in the Ohio State Penitentiary, a civilian prison rather than a military one.

Morgan served four months, then escaped with six of his men by tunneling through the floor with a stolen kitchen knife, climbing through a ventilation duct, digging up into the prison yard, climbing the wall, running to town, stealing a horse, eluding a five-thousand-dollar bounty on his head, and riding from Columbus, Ohio, to Richmond, Virginia, where he was received as a hero.

All of this contributed to Morgan's already amazing fame as a Southern hero, but it was pretty much downhill from there for him. He'd go on another raid in April 1864, but with most of his trusted horsemen either dead or captured, he had a bunch of unruly goons riding with him, and they torched warehouses and robbed a Federal bank of $59,000 of civilian money—an act that caused him to fall out of favor with the civilian populations in the South. He did actually manage to capture General Hobson, the man who had taken him in, but in true Morgan fashion the Confederate Thunderbolt let his old adversary go because he was just good like that.

Eventually the Federals had enough of this nonsense, and on the night of September 4, 1864, John Hunt Morgan was shot and killed in Greeneville, Tennessee, while trying to fight his way out of an ambush by Federal cavalry.

Lizzie Compton

When the Twenty-Fifth Michigan was doing battle with Morgan outside Green River, Kentucky, one of its front-line soldiers was fifteen-year-old Lizzie Compton, an orphaned Tennessee farm girl who'd lied about both her age and her gender in order to enlist in the Federal army. Already wounded by shrapnel at Antietam, the five-foot-tall Compton would repeatedly be discovered, be discharged, and then immediately reenlist, serving with seven different Union regiments during the course of the war.

Sounds of the Civil War

Music played a key role for both sides during the war, not only in the form of bugle calls to give orders from "charge" to "wake up" but also in regimental bands playing inspiring music to pump up the men to fight bravely in battle. From "Dixie" to "The Battle Hymn of the Republic," regimental bands blasted their music even as bullets ripped through their ranks, with the Federal army alone employing nearly thirty thousand musicians in its ranks.

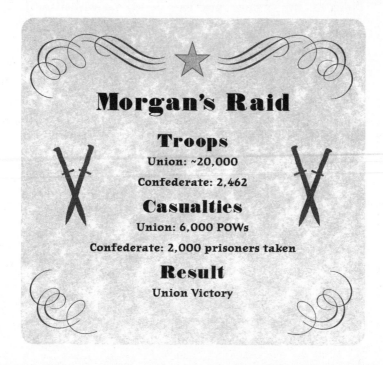

Morgan's Raid

Troops
Union: ~20,000
Confederate: 2,462

Casualties
Union: 6,000 POWs
Confederate: 2,000 prisoners taken

Result
Union Victory

Cavalrymen of the War

**If I cared for my life, I'd have lost it long ago.
Wanting to lose it, I can't throw it away.**

—Bloody Bill Anderson

Philip Kearny

The lone bright spot for the Army of the Potomac in the
early days of the war was the daring cavalry commander
Philip Kearny—a one-armed New Jersey boy who charged
his horse screaming into battle while carrying his saber in
one hand and holding his horse's reins in his teeth. Kearny
was the son of one of the men who founded the New York
Stock Exchange, but even though his family was totally
loaded, all this guy wanted to do was destroy his enemies
with a cavalry saber. After enlisting in the French army
in the early 1840s, Kearny fought in North Africa, but he
came back to the States in 1848 to join the US war against
Mexico, where he lost an arm to a cannonball. Amputation didn't even knock this guy out of action, however, and
after the war Kearny earned the French Legion d'Honneur
medal from Emperor Napoleon III for his actions fighting
on the side of France during the Italian Wars. When the
Civil War began, Kearny served under George McClellan,
whom he routinely accused of being either a coward or a

traitor. Consistently refusing orders to back down, fall back, or retreat, Kearny constantly urged his men to either hold their ground or attack until everything before them was dead, giving his men courage by leading from the front and assuring them, "Don't worry, boys—they'll all be firing at me!"

Benjamin Grierson

One of the Union's most famous raiders, Grierson was a music teacher from Pittsburgh who, ironically enough, always hated horses because one had kicked him in the head when he was a child. Famous for distracting Confederate troops from Grant's assault on Vicksburg, Grierson led 1,700 Illinois and Iowa cavalrymen eight hundred miles in seventeen days, traveling behind enemy lines burning storehouses, freeing slaves, and ripping up bridges and tracks in a raid so intense they made a John Wayne movie about it. After the war Grierson formed the Tenth US Cavalry, an African-American cavalry unit known as the "buffalo soldiers" that would earn fame and glory fighting out West against the American Indians.

Nathan Bedford Forrest

Loved by his men, despised by his enemies, and alternatively worshipped and demonized by history, Forrest was a hard-fighting, steel-toed warrior who rose through the ranks from private to lieutenant general, survived having twenty-nine horses killed out from underneath him, and always charged into combat at the head of his men armed with two .44-caliber Colt revolvers, a custom-made, ultra-heavy broadsword, and a double-barreled shotgun. Known for causing terror and destruction behind Union lines, this guy was so tough that one time one of his own junior officers pulled a pistol on him after an argument, so Forrest grabbed the gun right as the man pulled the trigger, held on to the weapon even as a .44-caliber bullet ripped into his hip at close range, dug into his pocket with his other hand, grabbed his pocketknife, pulled it out, unfolded the blade with his teeth, and then proceeded to stab the unfortunate lieutenant to death with a three-inch blade.

Bloody Bill Anderson

The most feared outlaw of the Civil War, Bloody Bill Anderson got his start robbing liquor stores and stealing horses owned by antislavery activists, but eventually he became a hardcore murderous guerrilla under the infamous William Clarke Quantrill. Commanding a crew of dangerous bushwhackers, Bloody Bill fought an unauthorized war for the Confederacy, attacking Union troops, trains, and supply depots across Missouri to disrupt their war operations. In August 1863, Anderson's three sisters were thrown into an old prison in Kansas City for supposedly collaborating with him. When the prison collapsed, killing one sister and permanently crippling another, Bloody Bill rode into the pro-Union town of Lawrence,

Kansas, looted the stores, pillaged, set fire to every building, and killed 150 men and boys (in Quantrill's words,
"every man big enough to hold a gun"). A few months after
that, the Raiders, who included infamous future outlaws
Frank James, Jesse James, and Cole Younger, took Fort
Blair from the Union. Anderson saw to it that every man
in the fort was killed, right down to the army band. Then
he scalped the bodies and hung the scalps from the saddle of his horse. He was killed in an ambush late in 1864,
when the terrifying outlaw fearlessly charged an entire
regiment of Union militia by himself.

Second Sabine Pass

The Davis Guards Hold the Line

*Jefferson County, Texas * September 8, 1863*

Who remembers how the iron-clad fleet came steaming up the river with nothing to oppose it but a mud fort armed with field guns and held by forty-two men; how its commander was asked by a comrade what was to be done, and suggested that they had better retreat; but how this gallant man said, "We will never retreat!" ...there are few in this audience who, if I asked them, could tell me who commanded at Sabine Pass. And yet, that battle at Sabine Pass was more remarkable than the battle of Thermopylae, and when it has orators and poets to celebrate it, will be so esteemed by mankind.

—Jefferson Davis, President, CSA

IN LATE **1863,** THINGS WERE GETTING WEIRD south of the US-Mexico border. About a year earlier, the French emperor Napoleon III had become a little upset about some unpaid debts the Mexican government failed to deal with, and instead of sending in debt collectors, he landed an army of thirty-five thousand Frenchmen at Veracruz, captured Mexico City, and cleared the way for an Austrian archduke dude named Maximilian to come in and become the emperor of Mexico. Because why not? Note that this was in complete violation of the Monroe Doctrine, an old-school American threat warning that if any Euro punks came into the Western Hemisphere thinking they could take over some Central or South American country, the United States would beat them senseless and dropkick them back across the Atlantic. But Napoleon figured the United States had its hands full with this Civil War thing, so if he wanted to deploy the French Foreign Legion and a couple corps of regular infantry on the doorstep of Mexico City and overthrow *el presidente*, there wasn't a whole heck of a lot ole Abe Lincoln was going to be able to do about it.

This, of course, worked out perfectly for the Rebels, who were desperate for help from France or anybody else who would listen. Jeff Davis and the Confederates immediately bought Napoleon a fruit basket and a pleasant greeting card, put on their swankiest suits, and tried to set up railroad lines between French-controlled Mexico and Confederate Texas. Here, finally, was the South's opportunity to find a way

around the Federal naval blockade—they'd bring all the supplies they needed in through Mexico, and there was nothing
Lincoln could do about it without starting an international
incident and going to war with both France and Mexico.

Understandably worried about the potential import of
European arms and weaponry across the Rio Grande, as well
as a mutual friendship/alliance between the Texans and the
French, Lincoln ordered his commander in the region, former governor of Massachusetts Nathaniel P. Banks, to take a
gigantic invasion force, attack Texas, cut it off from Mexico,
and conquer it in the name of the US of A.

Banks decided that the best way to launch his assault
would be by charging an amphibious invasion fleet through
Sabine Pass, the waterway that divides Texas from Louisiana. Not only was the river lightly guarded, with only a
single puny dirt fort to protect it, but it was right on the
state's only major railroad line linking Texas to the rest
of the Confederacy. Capturing the pass with a lightning
strike would cut Texas's lifeline, sever the only transporta-
tion route that linked Houston to New Orleans, and clear
the way for a complete conquest of the Lone Star State.
Banks appointed Captain Frederick Crocker, a salty former
Massachusetts whaling boat captain, to lead the mission.
Crocker had already led an attack on the pass a year earlier, capturing the town without losing a single man, but
the Union hadn't really seen the point in holding on to it at

that time, and eventually the Yankees pulled out and let the Rebels have it back.

Crocker, ready for just another day on the job, assembled his force—four heavily armed, highly maneuverable gunboats backed by eighteen heavy-assault transports containing six thousand men and five artillery batteries from the Union XIX Corps. His mission was simple: Subdue the small fort with overwhelming numbers, deploy his ground forces, and lay waste to Texas.

On the morning of September 8, 1863, the only thing standing between a fleet of twenty-two heavily armed Federal warships, six thousand veteran, professional Union soldiers, and thirty state-of-the-art artillery pieces preparing for a full-scale invasion and occupation of Texas was the battered, semifunctional, previously destroyed walls of Fort Griffin. This was a tiny mud structure equipped with a half-dozen old smoothbore cannons manned by forty-two Irish immigrants from Company F of the First Texas Heavy Artillery.

Commanded by a lieutenant named Richard Dowling, an Irishman who had opened a successful saloon in Houston after the potato famine and yellow fever killed off every single member of his family, the First Texas (better known as the Davis Guards) weren't exactly front-line troops. They were expendable resources, stuck in some backwater place that nobody actually expected to have to defend. Sure, they'd seen a little fighting already—at the Battle of Galveston they'd charged through knee-deep water and scaled ladders into an enemy fort despite heavy resistance, and a few months earlier they'd manned cannons on the CSS *Uncle Ben* when it attacked and captured two Federal gunboats. But these weren't men who woke up every morning expecting to have to fight for their lives against the entire Union XIX Corps with the fate of their home state hanging in the balance. Heck, Dowling wasn't even the full-time commander of Company F; he just happened to be there because the ranking officer had gone into the city to try to recruit more troops.

You can imagine the sight that Dowling looked out at on the morning of September 8. One of his sergeants, correctly

realizing that forty-two versus six thousand wasn't exactly good odds, suggested that, hey, maybe it made sense to get the heck out of there and run for their lives and never look back. Dowling assembled his men, told them the situation, and informed them that he refused to leave, even if it meant he was going to man every gun there himself.

His men stood by him. They cheered "Victory or Death!"— the same motto the Alamo's defenders had adopted when faced with similarly lopsided odds twenty-seven years earlier.

The first Federal warships steamed into the pass at about three thirty. Two gunboats—the *Clifton* and the *Granite City*—came up the Texas side of the river while another pair of vessels—the *Arizona* and the *Sachem*—charged up the Louisiana side. The *Clifton*, a converted Staten Island ferryboat decked out with eight cannons, packed full of Federal sharpshooters with state-of-the-art sniper rifles, and personally commanded by Captain Crocker, took the lead, opening fire with everything it had as soon as the Confederate fort was in its sights. Hammering Dowling and his men with explosive shells and covering them in churned-up dirt and swirling smoke, the *Clifton* bombarded the mud walls of Fort Griffin, blasting one of the fort's cannons right off its mounting and churning the air with enough shrapnel and gunpowder to keep Dowling and the Davis Guards suppressed while the rest of the Federal gunboats began their advance.

Dowling ordered his men not to fire.

Seeing that the coast was clear, the *Sachem* and the *Arizona* charged ahead. Their mission was to pull up across from the fort, hit it hard, and free up the *Clifton* and the *Granite City* so they could advance farther up the fort's side of the river, drop their troops, assault the fortress with overwhelming numbers, and hold it while the heavier troop transports rolled up and unloaded their men.

When the *Sachem* steamed to exactly 1,200 yards from Fort Griffin's walls, it passed a nondescript white-painted wooden stake poking up out of the water.

Seconds later, Fort Griffin's cannons sprang to life.

Richard Dowling, a founding member of what became the Houston Fire Department, might have been in charge of backwater conscripts languishing out on the far edges of the Confederacy, commanding a stupid little fort that had no expectation of ever having to fight off a large-scale Federal invasion force, but he was a man who took his job seriously. As it would turn out, he had spent every single day of his posting drilling his men in how to most effectively load, fire, and aim their guns as fast as possible, as well as how to adjust for trajectory and bullet drop and speed of approaching vehicles. To help them in this mission, he placed stakes indicating ranges in the water, and ensured that every man in his command could hit an approaching warship at any range that could be reached by his twenty-four- and thirty-two-pound cannons.

Once his five surviving guns were ready, his crews reloaded

and fired them almost twice as quickly as even the most experienced Confederate artillery crews.

And they didn't miss.

On the third or fourth round, the *Sachem* swerved to avoid the ultra-accurate fire and ended up running aground in a shallow oyster bed. The ship was now a sitting duck. The next cannon shell scored a direct hit on its boiler, blowing up the steam propulsion engine and showering the entire crew with face-searing sprays of scalding-hot steam. The *Arizona* rushed ahead, firing back at the fort, but when the ship's commander saw the entire crew of the *Sachem* leaping into the water as their ship exploded around them, the *Arizona* lost its nerve and turned around to run for it.

On the other side of the river, the *Granite City* and the *Clifton* continued their assault, speeding forward as fast as they could go, firing their guns into the fort, the *Clifton*'s snipers peering through their telescopic sights looking to pick off the gunners any time they popped their heads up.

Inside the fort, Dowling screamed for his men to stay down, load, fire, remember their training, push it to the limit, and all that other stuff that commanders yell to pump their troops up. With shrapnel, explosions, and bullets whizzing around in every direction, his men continued to work their guns with ruthless efficiency, even though most of the cannons were becoming so hot they were glowing red and were putting out so much heat they burned the fingerprints off of the men tasked with reloading them. Despite all this destruction swirling around them, with gunboats hurling dozens of rounds at them and an army of six thousand riflemen waiting in the wings, the Davis Guards fought on, their spirits bolstered by two ultra-brave local women, Kate Dorman and Sarah Vosburg, who utterly ignored almost certain death so that they could go up and down the battle line handing out doughnuts and coffee and whiskey to the men.

Captain Crocker, on board the *Clifton*, continued closing the distance to the fort, his forward swivel gun striking home, blasting one of the fort's five remaining cannons with a direct hit, sending the gun's crew diving for cover through a barrage of sniper rifle fire as their cannon exploded and burst into pieces behind them.

Seconds later, an accurate shot from one of Fort Griffin's four remaining cannons struck the steering on the *Clifton*, throwing her off course and sending her into a controlled spin. Crocker unleashed a broadside that raked Griffin with shot and shell, but Dowling's men, seeing a kill in their sights, put another round into *Clifton*'s boiler as well, detonating the ship's power plant into a vaporized cloud of steam. Dead in the water, Crocker continued to fire broadside after broadside, ordering the *Granite City* to get up there and unload her marines. The *Granite City* attempted to approach, but when her captain saw accurate rounds exploding on either side of him, he took one look at the crew of the *Clifton* abandoning

ship and he bolted for it so quickly that he ran himself and the
Arizona aground at the mouth of the pass, right into the
troop transports, two of which collided, and another that
ran aground and was forced to dump two hundred thousand
pounds of rations and two hundred mules in order to extricate
itself. The Union fleet, believing they had woefully underesti-
mated how many men and guns were at Fort Griffin, hauled
back to New Orleans and never returned to Sabine Pass.

In an hour and a half, Lieutenant Richard Dowling and
the forty-one men of the Davis Guards fired 130 rounds from
five cannons, working their guns so hard that the cannons
couldn't be fired for a day and a half after the battle. They had
grounded two Federal gunboats, damaged two more, inflicted
one hundred casualties, captured the Federal commander, sal-
vaged sixteen cannons from wrecked warships, and thwarted
an invasion of Texas by six thousand men. And they'd done it
without losing a single soldier. Combing the shores after the
battle, Dowling and his men also captured 350 Federal soldiers, which was no small feat of bluffing and ingenuity when
you consider that the Davis Guards only had forty-two guys.

Dowling and his men were immediately hailed as incredible heroes, not only by their commanders but by the residents
of the local town, all of whom were glad to have been spared
a Yankee occupation force. To honor the service of their brave
defenders, the women of the town smoothed off silver Mexican dollars, carved commemorative messages in them, put

them on a green ribbon to honor the Davis Guards' Irish heritage, and handed a medal to each man who had fought at the battle. When word of this got to Confederate president Jefferson Davis, he ensured that the Davis Guards' medal was formally approved by the Confederate Congress in Virginia. It would be the only medal ever to be officially awarded by the Confederate States of America.

No More Napoleon

The much-feared France–Texas pipeline never fully materialized, thanks in no small part to the fact that the Mississippi River was completely in Union hands and there was really no way to transport weapons or supplies from Texas to the rest of the Confederacy anyway. After the Civil War, the United States would finally be able to turn its attention to this Napoleon-in-Mexico nonsense. President Andrew Johnson sent plenty of aid, money, and weapons to Mexican rebels trying to overthrow Emperor Maximilian, and continued to put heavy political pressure on Napoleon to pull his troops out of there. Facing mounting resistance from world governments and the Mexican population, Napoleon would eventually withdraw French troops from Mexico. Without the support of his European masters, Emperor Maximilian would be defeated, captured, and executed by firing squad in 1867.

The Second Battle of Sabine Pass

Sailors/Troops

Union: 6,000

Confederate: 42

Casualties

Union: 100 killed,
350 captured

Confederate: 0

Result

Confederate Victory

The World in 1864

I've already mentioned the French invasion of Mexico, but a lot of exciting things happened in the world in 1864, and not just because it was a leap year or because it was the major turning point of the outcome of the American Civil War. The British Empire was at the height of its power, forging an empire that spanned from Canada to India, with Queen Victoria's redcoats battling Ashanti warriors in Africa, and overseeing the construction of the Suez Canal in Egypt. There was still the problem of the Irish continually rebelling, sure, but the British were feeling pretty good about themselves after having beaten down a humongous rebellion in India in 1857 and whipping up on the Russians in the Crimean War in 1856, a multination conflict highlighted by the infamous "Charge of the Light Brigade."

The Russian empire, which had just had its butt kicked in Crimea, wasn't quite so happy. They'd been trying to grab land from the crumbling Ottoman Turkish empire, but their ambitions had been thwarted by an angry force of Turks, Brits, and French. Now the Russians were retiring to deal with internal problems and were so freaked out about British aggression that they sold Alaska to the United States in 1867 for seven million dollars to prevent the Canadians from capturing it. Russian tsar Alexander II had just freed the serfs (basically Russian peasant slaves) from their servitude in 1861, and the government was trying to deal with the repercussions of that action. Ominously and somewhat related to this, German economist Karl Marx's book *Das Kapital* would be published that year as well, laying the foundation for the Communist revolution that would overthrow the tsar fifty years later.

Speaking of Germany, it still wasn't even a country yet. It was just a big group of states that spoke German, the most powerful of which was a place called Prussia. By 1864, a Prussian politician named Otto von Bismarck was making a meteoric rise to power, and he'd become chancellor of the North German Confederation in 1867. A couple of wars and a bit of diplomacy later, the "Iron Chancellor" would unify Germany under one emperor and generate enough hard feelings in the process to set Europe on the path to World War I.

Italy wasn't a country yet either, but a freedom fighter named Giuseppe Garibaldi was to take care of that as well. Fighting a series of wars against Austrians and French (who weren't particularly interested in Italy becoming a country—they'd been burned by that whole Roman Empire thing a few years earlier), Garibaldi would unify his country by 1866.

Meanwhile South America was basically becoming a massive war zone, with the tiny country of Paraguay foolishly going to war with Argentina, Brazil, and Uruguay all at the same time. It didn't end well for Paraguay, which lost nearly 60 percent of the population and was utterly destroyed.

Over in Asia the Chinese were in the middle of the single deadliest civil war in human history, the Taipeng Rebellion. Basically, some guy named Hong Xiuquan came out and said he was the younger brother of Jesus sent to overthrow the corrupt Chinese imperial system. The Qing Dynasty emperor of China disagreed, and an estimated *twenty million people died.*

Japan was in upheaval as well, although they were still mostly using awesome samurai swords rather than guns at this point. The Japanese, angry about the shogun allowing Westerners to come into their country and mess things up, were in the process of overthrowing the Tokugawa shogunate and reinstating the emperor as the true source of power in Japan, a revolution known as the Meiji Restoration. With an imperial decree to "Revere the Emperor, Destroy the Barbarians," provinces were rebelling, katana-swinging samurai were killing Westerners wherever they could find them, and vicious back-alley street sword fighting between the shogun's men and Imperial forces were a nightly occurrence.

So...yeah. Good times all around.

The Rock of Chickamauga

George Henry Thomas

Catoosa County, Georgia ✳ *September 19–20, 1863*

> This army can't retreat. Gentlemen,
> I know of no better place to die than right here.
>
> —Major General George H. Thomas, US Army

HIS FRIENDS HAD LABELED HIM A TRAITOR. His home state forbade him from ever returning. His superior officers doubted his loyalty. His own family disowned him.

Nobody would have expected a Virginia general to be the man to save the Union army from annihilation in the second-largest battle of the Civil War.

Born on a decent-sized plantation in Southampton County, Virginia, in July 1816, George Henry Thomas was just fifteen years old when a local slave named Nat Turner banded together with other slaves on their plantation, killed their masters, and began a violent rebellion that left over sixty people dead in just a few days. In the opening hours of the rebellion, Turner and his men were going from house to house in Southampton County, killing white families with everything from machetes to fence posts and freeing their black slaves in an effort to incite a widespread uprising. When Thomas got word of what was going on, he first brought his widowed mother and his sisters to a safe hiding place in the forest, then went on a wild midnight ride to warn his neighbors of the impending danger.

Thomas was appointed to West Point in 1840 (where he was a roommate of William Tecumseh Sherman) and enlisted in the US Army as an artillerist immediately out of school. He served with honor for fifteen years, doing battle with Seminole warriors in the knee-deep swamps of Florida, battling tomahawk-slinging Apache in Texas, and directing cannon fire against Mexican Army soldiers at the Battles of Buena Vista and Monterrey during the Mexican-American War. After a four-year stint as a professor of artillery at West Point, Thomas went back into the field, serving as a major in the Second Cavalry Regiment, where he was third-in-command behind Lieutenant Colonel Robert E. Lee and Colonel Albert Sidney Johnston and somehow survived taking an arrow wound to the face while battling American Indians in 1860.

When the Civil War broke out a year later, George Henry Thomas had a decision to make. His home state had seceded. His two commanding officers, both Southerners, declared their loyalty to their states and resigned their commissions, and the Confederate government had already offered him a post as overall commander of all Rebel artillery. The Federal government was calling for troops to battle the Rebellion and needed experienced men to lead them. Choosing the North would be a betrayal of his state, his people, his family, and everyone he grew up with, and would put him in a position where he would need to fight and kill men who had once been his friends and neighbors. Choosing the South would be treason against his beloved country, a disgrace to the blue uniform he'd proudly worn for fifteen years, and a violation of the oath he'd taken to defend his country "against all enemies foreign and domestic."

Thomas chose his country, his uniform, and his duty as an officer in the United States Army. His sisters never spoke to him again.

Even though his superiors doubted this Virginian's loyalty to the Union cause, they were hard up for experienced commanders, and Thomas was put in charge of a Pennsylvania Infantry brigade at Manassas in 1861. He was then transferred out west, where he defeated his former boss Albert Sidney Johnston at the Battle of Mill Springs in 1862, and proved his allegiance to the cause with stalwart defensive fighting at

Shiloh, Perryville, and a half dozen other battlefields ranging from Kentucky to Tennessee. At the Battle of Stones River, after Confederate assaults wiped out the Union forces and threatened to completely tear his corps asunder, Thomas assembled every one of his subordinate officers, looked each one in the eyes, and told them that this army was going to hold the line or die where they stood. Pumped up by Thomas's fearlessness, the Yankees stormed into the freezing-cold December snow, clinging to their position in a cedar forest against countless attacks by enemy forces, somehow keeping the Union army from being split in half despite overwhelming enemy pressure.

The heroic stand that gave Thomas his lasting fame came in September 1863, when, surrounded on three sides and backed up against a river, he single-handedly took on the entire sixty-five-thousand-man Confederate army with just a few thousand guys and somehow managed to prevent them from utterly annihilating the Union army of the Cumberland.

The Battle of Chickamauga was a last-ditch Confederate effort to make up for backbreaking losses at Vicksburg and Gettysburg and turn the tables back against the North. With their sights set on retaking Chattanooga, the South concentrated everything they had on attacking and destroying the Army of the Cumberland under William S. Rosecrans, launching a colossal onslaught on the Union army in the second-biggest engagement of the entire war.

George Henry Thomas's corps found themselves in the middle of the action, defending the Union center, fighting off everything from a daylight assault by Nathan Bedford Forrest's dismounted cavalry to a ferocious night attack led by Patrick Cleburne, an Irish-born British army vet and part-time lawyer who once survived a street fight in Helena, Arkansas, by taking a bullet in the back, drawing his revolver, turning around, and killing the man who'd just shot him. Cleburne's men, who were just as tough as he was, charged through the dense Georgia woods at dusk and continued their attack after dark, their shadowy figures backlit by the raging fires of the forest, the battlefield illuminated only by the muzzle flashes of musketry and artillery. Still, the Union line held, its defenders firing their rifles into the darkness before them.

The next morning the Confederates picked up where they had left off the night before, launching a substantial series of assaults against Thomas's position. Cleburne, who already had four teeth knocked out after being shot in the face at the Battle of Richmond, once again launched a series of charges uphill straight on toward Thomas. A separate division, under the command of John C. Breckinridge—the former vice president of the United States and a man who just received one-third of the popular vote in the 1860 presidential election that put Abraham Lincoln in power—tried to sweep around

Thomas's left and attack him from the side. Thomas, masterfully positioning his troops despite being hammered from two directions at once, somehow held the line, throwing back the Rebels by counterattacking them every time they broke through his lines, his men barely clinging to their trenches by their fingernails.

Then things got worse. Elsewhere on the battlefield, twenty-three thousand shrieking Confederate soldiers under the command of General James Longstreet, fresh off a train from Northern Virginia, broke through the Union right, opening a black hole of misery that sent half the Union army—including overall army commander William Rosecrans—running for their lives. Now all that remained of the Union Army of the Cumberland was George Henry Thomas and the nineteen thousand men of XIV Corps, surrounded by Rebel forces before him and on both his flanks, outnumbered three to one against a foe that could smell victory like it was a Thanksgiving turkey.

Clinging to his position with a ragtag band of exhausted Union soldiers pieced together from units that had already been annihilated, Thomas repositioned his decimated forces. When gaps opened across his lines, he ordered his few remaining reserve troops to charge bayonets-first into breaches before they were flooded with a seemingly endless horde of Southerners who would stop at nothing to destroy his entire command. His brave troops, running on forty-eight hours

without sleep and having sustained the brunt of the destruction for two full days, still refused to budge. They resolved to
fight as long as they could and buy the fleeing Union army
time to get out of there and regroup. Thomas was going to
hold this ground until someone buried him underneath it.

Somehow, incredibly, despite defending a hill against the
entire Rebel Army of Tennessee, George Henry Thomas
held his position throughout the day, finally slipping his
wounded, exhausted men out of there under the cover of
darkness and marching them back to Chattanooga. For saving the Union army from complete destruction, Northern
newspapers would forever refer to him after this as "the
Rock of Chickamauga."

When Thomas fell back to Chattanooga he was given command of the Army of the Cumberland, because that Rosecrans guy was worthless, and Thomas soon found himself
besieged by the Confederates. He held out for a while until he
could be reinforced by Grant and Sherman, who then ordered
Thomas's depleted corps to launch a limited assault on the
Confederate center to test their defenses. Grant figured
Thomas's men were demoralized and exhausted, and didn't
expect much.

They failed to appreciate how righteously angry Thomas
and his men were, and how eagerly they wanted retribution for the horror they'd withstood at Chickamauga.
Instead of a wimpy holding action, George Henry Thomas

personally led twenty-three thousand men in a full-scale
attack charging up a forty-five-degree incline into Confederate trenches packed with tens of thousands of riflemen and over a hundred cannons. Grant and Sherman,
observing the battle from the nearby heights, watched in
disbelief as Thomas's warriors raced up the hill. As their
commanders stared openmouthed, the Army of the Cumberland swept across the Rebel trenches, forced the enemy
off the hill with the points of their bayonets, took their

cannons, turned the guns around, and advanced the Stars and Stripes all the way to the other side of the mountain in a sea of blue-coated retribution. The Rebel army broke and ran for it. They never returned.

George Henry Thomas was given command of half of Sherman's forces during the Atlanta Campaign, then squared off against his former West Point student John Bell Hood when the Confederates once again attempted to reverse the tide of the war, first at the Battle of Franklin, when Thomas turned back an assault that was twice the size of Pickett's Charge, and then counterattacking with a savagery that effectively blasted the Confederate army in the West out of existence for the rest of the war.

George Henry Thomas survived the war and was revered as a hero by the Northern media. He spent his later years commanding Federal forces in California, where he died in 1870. The State of Virginia refused to allow him to be buried there, so he was laid to rest with his wife's family in New York.

The Thirteen-Year-Old Sergeant

During the retreat from Chickamauga, one Confederate colonel rushing through Union lines came across eleven-year-old Johnny Clem, an Ohio boy who had run away from home at the age of nine to enlist in the Twenty-Second Michigan Infantry as a drummer boy. The colonel failed to have respect for the fact that this kid was a cold-blooded killer and a veteran of every battle from Shiloh to Chickamauga, or that he was packing heat. When the colonel demanded a surrender, Clem quick-drew his pistol, shot the colonel, and took *him* prisoner instead. Clem would be a thirteen-year-old sergeant by the end of the war, making him the youngest non-commissioned officer in American history. He graduated high school in 1870, got married in 1875, and retired as a brigadier general in 1915, a fifty-five-year veteran of the US military.

The Battle of Chickamauga

Troops

Union: 60,000 • Confederate: 65,000

Casualties

Union: 16,170 • Confederate: 18,454

Result

Confederate Victory

Union Nurse

Mary Edwards Walker

November 23–25, 1863 ✳ Chattanooga, Tennessee

> Tables about breast high had been erected upon which the screaming victims were having legs and arms cut off. The surgeons and their assistants, stripped to the waist and bespattered with blood, stood around, some holding the poor fellows while others, armed with long, bloody knives and saws, cut and sawed away with frightful rapidity, throwing the mangled limbs on a pile nearby as soon as removed.
>
> —Lieutenant Colonel W. W. Blackford, First Virginia Cavalry

DETONATING ARTILLERY SHELLS AND THE NON-stop rattling of musketry menacingly rumbled in the distance, barely audible over the groans and agonizing cries of dying men as droves of new arrivals steadily flooded into the ordinary, single-family home that was now being utilized as a front-line field hospital. Horse-drawn ambulance carts packed full of trauma victims lined the driveway to a grisly facility that

mashed together a barely serviceable emergency room, operating room, and morgue into a painfully typical three-bedroom
house on the outskirts of Chattanooga, Tennessee. The hospital's overworked, exhausted nurses desperately tried to triage
the wounded between those who were possibly treatable and
those who weren't going to make it.

Outside the city walls, the Union army, pushed back to
Chattanooga following their thrashing at Chickamauga, was
making a tenacious stand to hold the city against a rabid
Confederate counterattack. Forty-six thousand men of
Braxton Bragg's Army of Tennessee were entrenched on the
heights overlooking the critical strategic rail and communications center, with the Union forces backed up against the
Tennessee River, but now an assault led by General George
Henry Thomas was rushing up a steep ridge right into enemy
positions that included 112 cannons, and were taking murderous fire from the enemy in an all-out attempt to clobber the
Confederates' defensive positions and break out of the siege.
Those wounded soldiers who were lucky enough to find their
way back to friendly lines found themselves here, in a stinking, unsterilized makeshift hospital surrounded by malaria-
infected men and saw-wielding surgeons practicing a particular brand of medicine that had more in common with
medieval torture than anything resembling a modern-day
visit to the pediatrician. Their only consolations were a cup
of cold water and the soothing voices of nurses trying to

comfort them and ease their pain in some small way.

During the Civil War, over ten thousand women worked as nurses in field hospitals across the war zone.

Mary Edwards Walker of the Fifty-Second Ohio Volunteer Infantry was the only one who served as a surgeon. She's also the only woman in history to ever receive the Medal of Honor, the highest award for military bravery offered by the United States of America.

Walker was roughly a hundred and fifty years ahead of her time. Routinely criticized by women and men alike for her desire to wear men's clothing (at a time when men's clothing basically meant any article of clothing that allowed you to walk through doorways or work in any capacity whatsoever), Walker paid her own way through Geneva Medical College (now called Syracuse Medical College) in 1855, becoming just the second woman in American history to complete physician training and work as a doctor. When the Civil War broke out in 1861, Walker had already been running her own private practice for six years, but even though there were just eighty-six licensed surgeons in the Union army at the start of the hostilities, she was still turned away by every recruiting officer she approached. Undeterred, the twenty-nine-year-old surgeon signed on as a volunteer nurse, working on the front lines at the First Battle of Bull Run, then working as an unpaid volunteer surgeon at Indiana Hospital later that year.

Walker continued her practice of "I'll just show up wherever people are dying and see if they'll maybe let me help fix them for free," volunteering at the Battle of Fredericksburg in 1862, performing front-line operations, and taking control of a medical train that was ferrying wounded men back to Washington. Her skills at slicing and dicing men in the name of science so impressed Union general Ambrose Burnside that the Federal commander nominated her for a commission. At first she met with the resistance she was so used to encountering, but thanks to Burnside's recommendation, she was finally commissioned as an assistant surgeon in the

Fifty-Second Ohio Volunteer Infantry, issued a US Army surgeon's uniform, and sent to Tennessee to help treat wounded and dying men during the siege of Chattanooga. She would be the only woman in the war to receive this honor.

Now, in order to fully appreciate how intense the job of a Civil War surgeon actually was, try to think of it as something of a cross between the Spanish Inquisition and a butcher shop. Since artillery shells, canister fire, and cannonballs typically resulted in the instant, untreatable, and horrific death of anyone unlucky enough to be standing in front of a cannon muzzle, the majority of Civil War surgical cases were from gunshot wounds caused by a .58-caliber minié ball. This was a soft metal, mostly hollow, incredibly heavy projectile over half an inch in diameter that was shaped very much like a modern bullet. It hit so hard that any bone it came in contact with shattered like a fluorescent lightbulb being smacked against a brick wall. The minié ball also mushroomed on impact much like a modern-day hollow-point bullet, expanding to about an inch in width and ripping through muscles, blood vessels, organs, and all of those other important things that people keep inside their skin.

Because there was no such thing as organ transplantation, internal surgery, or blood transfusions, if a soldier got hit in the head, chest, or abdomen, he had a 90 percent chance of death; all anyone could do for the poor sucker was give him morphine and water and find a shady tree for him to sit under until he died. Wounds to the arms and legs had better odds, however, which is why fully three-quarters of surgeries performed during the war were amputations of these appendages.

Here's how it worked: After a guy got shot, he had forty-eight hours to get his arm cut off with an unsterilized hacksaw or he was probably going to die a painful death from gangrene. You, as the doctor, working in terrible conditions at someone's kitchen counter, would slosh the blood off the operating table with a bucket, get the guy up there, then you'd have a couple minutes to figure out what kind of shape he was in. If his arm wasn't broken, he might be okay—you could just wash it out, slap a tourniquet on there, and move on to the next guy. If it was fractured beyond repair, you'd need to operate, because medical tech wasn't advanced enough to do anything else about it. One of your nurses would anesthetize the dude with a chloroform-soaked rag (if it was available—in some field hospitals all you got was a shot of whiskey and a bullet to bite down on) until he was unconscious, then you'd have to stitch the broken artery closed with a needle and thread, dig the bullet out of there with your forceps, cut through the muscle with a sharp knife, saw through the bone with your hacksaw, tie off the arteries with another piece of thread, and then sew it all shut into a stump.

A good surgeon could perform the operation in under ten minutes. And he'd do it dozens of times in a row, all while the city was being pounded with artillery shells and stray bullets

were slamming into the walls around him. Clara Barton recalled working on a guy in the hospital tent at Antietam and having a stray bullet pass through the tent and through the sleeve of her dress and then kill the patient right in front of her (which, honestly, may have been a more humane way to go). Back before we knew you had to sterilize your equipment between patients, almost 25 percent of people who underwent amputation surgery ended up dying from infected wounds.

Saving human lives by performing barbaric work with her bone saw under hellish conditions in the middle of a raging war zone as bullets and artillery shrapnel ripped through the skies around her, Mary Edwards Walker continued working as a front-line surgeon throughout the three-day Battle of Chattanooga. After a heroic, unlikely charge by George Henry Thomas's men broke the Confederate position and sent Bragg retreating back to Georgia, Walker continued her work, not only assisting wounded Federal troops but also crossing enemy lines and providing medical care to Confederate troops and civilians in Tennessee and Georgia.

On one of these trips to Georgia to aid sick and injured civilians, Walker was ambushed by Confederate pickets, who found her in her Union uniform carrying two pistols and arrested her as a spy, a detail that may or may not actually have been true (we can't prove it either way). Her captors, who noted in their report that she argued "enough for a regiment of men," recommended sending her to a lunatic asylum for being a woman doctor, but instead she was sent to Richmond and thrown in a jail for Federal prisoners of war. After she spent four months in horrifying conditions in the POW camp, Walker was sent back to Yankee lines as part of a prisoner exchange. (She later confessed that she was very proud to have been traded straight up for a male Confederate surgeon.)

Walker was sent back to the Union army, where she was attached to Sherman's army during the Atlanta Campaign. After the Battle of Atlanta, she was appointed chief surgeon at a women's military prison in Louisville, Kentucky, where she served until the end of the war. After her service, Walker collected an Army pension, wrote a couple books, became a women's suffrage activist, founded a weird commune, and got arrested a couple times for wearing pants instead of a dress.

During her time in the Union army, Dr. Mary Edwards Walker had been recommended for promotion both by General George Henry Thomas and by General William Tecumseh Sherman. Since she technically wasn't a uniformed service member, these requests for promotion could not be granted, but in honor of her service Mary Edwards Walker was awarded the Congressional Medal of Honor in 1866. Of the 1.8 million women who have served in the US military, she is the only one to ever receive the award. The federal government tried to go back on this in 1917 when it changed the guidelines for the Medal of Honor, stipulating that the medal could only be awarded for actions that occurred in combat, and stripped nine hundred people—including Dr. Walker—of their awards. Walker, obviously, told them to get bent—she wore the medal until her death in 1919. It was officially reinstated by order of the president in 1977.

Medal of Honor

The Medal of Honor was the first, and to this day highest, award for military valor offered by the US government. Created in 1861 as an American version of Britain's Victoria Cross, it was originally issued simply for "gallantry in action," but the circumstances for receiving it have been considerably tightened up since. Some 1,200 medals were awarded during the Civil War, but once restrictions got tighter in 1917, about 911 of them were revoked.

Dog Tags

In the chaos of hospitals and battlefields it was almost impossible to identify individual soldiers among the heaps of dead. Many troops, hoping to be ID'd so their families back home could have closure, started carrying metal or wood pendants etched with their name, unit, and next of kin, hoping that if they were to die in combat nobody would forget who they were. The US military would expand this practice prior to World War I with the issuing of individual ID badges known as "dog tags."

Battle Above the Clouds

One of the most literally over-the-top actions during the Battle of Chattanooga was the so-called Battle Above the Clouds. With Lookout Mountain anchoring the Confederate flank, General "Fighting Joe" Hooker was ordered to assault the position, get his troops atop the 2,390-foot-tall peak, and then sight artillery down on Missionary Ridge. Hooker's men dutifully charged ahead, scaling the mountaintop through thick fog and clouds, fighting their way to the summit and capturing over a thousand Rebel soldiers in the process. Since historians love to keep track of ridiculously obscure details regarding the Civil War, it bears mentioning that this was the highest elevation of any battle of the war.

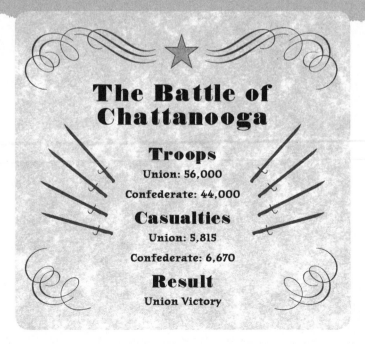

The Battle of Chattanooga

Troops

Union: 56,000

Confederate: 44,000

Casualties

Union: 5,815

Confederate: 6,670

Result

Union Victory

Grant Versus Lee

The Overland Campaign

Northern Virginia * May 4–June 12, 1864

> The art of war is simple enough. Find out where your enemy is. Get at him as soon as you can. Strike him as hard as you can, and keep moving on.

—Lieutenant General Ulysses S. Grant, commanding officer, US Army

ANY TIME YOU HAVE HEROES, LEADERS, AND warriors as ever victorious and unquestionably hardcore as Robert E. Lee and Ulysses S. Grant battling each other on opposite sides of an epic, life-or-death struggle with the fate of countries and the world hanging in the balance, it's only a matter of time until everything comes down to one final ultimate showdown between the two armies' greatest champions.

In the Civil War, this showdown began in May 1864, when Union general Ulysses S. Grant—the man behind virtually every single major Federal victory of the war—received his official promotion to overall commander of the US Army and was shipped out to Washington, DC, to finally do battle with Confederate general Robert E. Lee and his vaunted, almost unbeatable Army of Northern Virginia.

The showdown between these two men would be brutal, vicious, and decisive. Two men were going into battle, and only one army would emerge victorious.

Born Hiram Ulysses Grant in Point Pleasant, Ohio, Grant allegedly changed his name to Ulysses Simpson when he enrolled in West Point, mostly because he didn't want cadets harassing him for having the initials HUG. A master horseman and hard-nosed fighter, Grant was a hero of the Mexican-American War, when he served under Zachary Taylor and Winfield Scott, but after the war he was stationed way out on the West Coast. Grant eventually resigned from the army because he was depressed about having to be so far away from his wife for such extended periods of time. Once out of the military, he ran a farm into the ground, lost his job as a bill collector in St. Louis, and was eventually forced to take a terrible-paying retail job working as a thirty-nine-year-old clerk behind the counter at his dad's saddle shop in Galena, Illinois. Not the sort of background you'd expect from the eighteenth president of the United States of America.

When the Civil War started, Grant left his wife and four kids at home and joined the Twenty-First Illinois Volunteer Infantry. He rose through the ranks quickly, captured Fort Henry early in the war, then blew everyone's socks off in 1862 when he disobeyed direct orders, marched his fifteen thousand men to the Confederate stronghold of Fort Donelson, and somehow forced the unconditional surrender of almost the entire twenty-one-thousand-man garrison, scoring the first major Union victory of the entire Civil War. A few months later he weathered the storm at Shiloh and turned a potentially miserable defeat into an unbelievable Federal victory. Never one to back down from a good fight, Grant continually led his troops farther and farther into enemy territory, coordinated the brilliant amphibious attack that captured Vicksburg, split the Confederacy in half along the Mississippi River, then destroyed Braxton Bragg's Army of Tennessee at Chattanooga. Sure, he drank too much and smoked so many cigars he eventually died from it, but he was also the most tenacious warrior the Federal army had on its payroll, and that's the sort of thing that helps a guy overlook his commander's personal vices. When warned by a subordinate of Grant's love of most things booze-related, Abraham Lincoln once famously remarked, "Tell me the brand of whiskey he drinks. I would like to send a barrel of it to my other generals."

So when the time came to face Robert E. Lee once more, Grant was the obvious choice to lead the operation.

Reduced to about sixty-five thousand troops, the Army of
Northern Virginia had been battered pretty severely at Gettysburg, but they were far from dead, and, more importantly,
they'd still never been defeated on their home turf. Taking
the fight to them would be no easy task. Grant knew this, but
this was a man who loved a good death match, and he wasn't
interested in doing anything other than using the North's
utterly unbalanced advantage in manpower and equipment to
grind Lee's forces into dust until nothing stood between Abe
Lincoln and Richmond, Virginia. When several high-ranking
members of the Army of the Potomac shared some Lee-related
horror stories with their newly arrived commander, Grant's
response was simple: "I am heartily tired hearing about what
Lee is going to do. Some of you think he is suddenly going to
turn a double somersault and land in our rear and on both
our flanks at the same time. Go back to your commands and
try to think what we are going to do ourselves, rather than
what Lee is going to do."

The sixth invasion of Virginia began in May 1864, when U. S.
Grant marched 120,000 soldiers across the Rapidan River with
one objective—take Richmond, destroy Lee, and end the war.

Lee's troops were entrenched south of the Rapidan. When
he heard reports that Grant was leading the Army of the
Potomac right into the heart of the now infamous Wilderness,
he resorted to the tactics that made him famous—he attacked.
Advancing through the same terrain where he had demolished

Federal forces at Chancellorsville, Lee attempted to re-create his famous victory by once again splitting his forces. He positioned Old Baldy Ewell's and A. P. Hill's corps to pin Grant's advancing columns in place, then sent Longstreet on an end run designed to get around the Union and attack them from the rear.

It was a brilliant tactic that would have worked to perfection against every other inept commander the Army of the Potomac ever had. The only difference is that this time Lee was facing a warrior who was just as gutsy as he was. A man who refused to back down. Instead of sitting around letting a force half his size pin him down so that Longstreet could run around the flank and punch him in the kidneys, Grant simply ordered his men to attack with everything they had.

On May 5, 1864, Union troops rolled through the ultra-dense, seemingly impassable forests of the Wilderness, which at this point was now creepy as anything because it was littered with the bones of men who perished on the same grounds during the Battle of Chancellorsville just a year earlier. Shock troops under Winfield Scott Hancock's II Corps sprinted through the black smoke and uncontrolled forest fires now ravaging the Wilderness, driving the Rebels back in disorder. Longstreet called off his end run and rushed back to seal the breach, reaching the battlefield in time to see Robert E. Lee personally on the front lines, repositioning artillery batteries and giving orders to infantry regiments in full view of the much-feared Vermont Brigade, which spearheaded the Union attack. The battle was a stalemate, with the Confederates losing eleven thousand men and the Union suffering eighteen thousand casualties.

This, if you'll recall, is the point in the campaign where virtually every other Union commander in the Army of the Potomac's history packed up his troops and ran back to Washington with his tail between his legs.

So when Ulysses Simpson Grant turned his horse south and issued the order for his troops to pack up their gear, grab their rifles, and circle around the Confederates' right flank to block off their escape route back to Richmond, his enlisted soldiers and sergeants gave a huge cheer—*finally*, a guy who would fight. A guy who was not going to run for it at the first sign of trouble. The battle cry "On to Richmond!" erupted all along the Federal lines, eventually getting so intense that Grant himself had to silence it so that the men didn't accidentally give up their positions to Lee's scouts.

Eager to outmaneuver his nemesis, Grant raced south toward Spotsylvania Court House, a crossroads between the Wilderness and Richmond. Lee realized what was going on and sent troops there. His nephew, Fitzhugh Lee, arrived first with his cavalry regiments and slowed down the advancing Federal columns by barricading the road with chopped-down trees, and by the time the Union arrived at Spotsylvania,

Rebel troops had already dug in defensive positions. Both sides moved into position and prepared to slug it out once more.

On May 9 and 10, not even a week after the Wilderness, Grant launched another series of unsuccessful assaults, sending his men toward an intricate, ultra-intense series of fortifications that included man-sized, World War I–style trenches, hidden rifle pits, and camouflaged pieces of field artillery hidden behind walls of earth and wood. While none of these attacks were successful, Grant did realize that there was a weak point in the Rebel line, and he intended to exploit it.

At four AM on the morning of May 12, 1864, advanced columns of Winfield Scott Hancock's II Corps came marching ominously out of the rain-swept fog, their war drums and boots pounding like a freight train. Leaving the safety of the tree line in a full attack, twenty thousand Federal troops, mostly Northeasterners from New York, New Jersey, and Pennsylvania, unleashed a mighty battle cry and ran right into a sea of bullets. The Federals poured over the Confederate lines, capturing twenty-six cannons and two full divisions of Confederate troops, including the famous Stonewall Brigade.

Lee, seeing the utter destruction of his army flash before his eyes, personally led the counterattack, sending whatever troops he could muster immediately into the fray. With rain pouring down in sheets so thick it got the black powder wet and rendered most muskets unfireable, the Rebel counterattack met three corps of Union troops head-on in no-holds-barred, close-range combat so brutal even Gettysburg veterans would refer to it as the most vicious fighting they had ever seen.

The fight for the "Bloody Angle" lasted twenty hours, men fighting with punches, knives, clubbed rifles, and bayonets until four AM the next morning. Fires raged throughout the lines. Trees took so many bullets that they fell over like they'd been chainsawed. Ewell's corps, reduced to six thousand men, retook the lines, held, and pushed the Union out.

Yet, once again, Grant refused to quit. He just moved south and east, trying to cut Lee off from Richmond. The two forces met again at the Battle of Cold Harbor, just fifteen miles outside downtown Richmond. Lee, backed up against his capital with just sixty thousand men, many of them inexperienced troops scraped together from garrisons and other postings throughout the Confederacy, dug a formidable series of trenches, but Grant didn't back down. He was like a boxer who had been working the body for six rounds, and, with an assembled army of 110,000 troops positioned within spitting distance from the Confederate White House, he was going to go for the knockout blow. On June 3, 1864, Grant ordered an all-out assault on the Confederate position—every single man he had.

The Rebels, forged by four years of nonstop warfare, held their ground, firing straight into the Yankees with every gun they could bring to bear. The attack—as was the case with

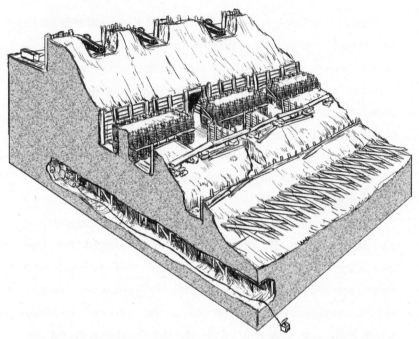

Earthworks like these appeared up and down both lines as the campaign progressed.

most assaults during the Civil War—was a suicide charge. Seven thousand Union soldiers were killed and wounded in four hours of fighting. It was one of the bloodiest slugfests of the entire war. Hancock, in yet another display of fearless bravado, was the only man to reach the Rebel trenches, but a counterattack drove him back. One Southern officer, watching the battle, remarked about Grant's tactics, "We have met a man this time who either does not know when he is whipped or who cares not if he loses his whole army."

Stubborn and determined, Ulysses S. Grant still refused to back down. Just as before, he maneuvered south and east, this time crossing the James River with ferries and pontoons and bringing his forces around to the southeastern side of Richmond. Lee, once again stuck having to react rather than attack, entrenched his forces outside the city of Petersburg—the only railroad station supplying Richmond, and the only source of food, weapons, and supplies for Lee's entire army. Under no circumstances could he lose this city.

Grant, however, had no intention of wasting more soldiers on stupid assaults. He simply took his one hundred thousand men, surrounded Petersburg, and dug thirty miles of entrenchments around the city. In one month of fighting, his Army of the Potomac had suffered sixty thousand dead and wounded while inflicting just thirty-five thousand casualties on the Confederates. Called a "butcher" by Northern newspapers for simply hurling wave after wave of his men into the Rebel meat grinder, Grant had nevertheless done what no other Union commander had ever done—he'd dictated the war to Robert E. Lee. And now he had the Rebels on their heels.

The 52,000 beleaguered, exhausted troops of Lee's army were now backed into a corner with nowhere to maneuver. They couldn't replace their losses, their already meager supply lines were in danger of being completely cut off, and they were now facing an enemy unlike anything they had ever seen before.

The two great generals would stare across their fortifications at each other for *nine months*, neither side daring an attack. The war had evolved from the old-school, open-field, close-order maneuverings of ancient gunpowder battles to the grim, bleak, desolate, scorched-earth trench warfare that would characterize World War I.

Bye-Bye, Burnside

The most interesting part of the nine-month siege of Petersburg took place on July 30, 1864, when Ambrose Burnside ordered men from the Forty-Eighth Pennsylvania, a unit comprised mostly of coal miners, to dig a 511-foot-long mine underneath the Confederate trench network, pack it with eight thousand pounds of explosives, and then blow a gigantic gaping hole in the Rebel lines. The mine and explosion was a success, blasting a thirty-foot-deep, 170-foot-long crater in the earth that ripped apart the Rebel trench system and killed three hundred men, but the ensuing assault into the breach was a disaster—Union troops went into the crater instead of around it, got pinned down in the hole by Confederate artillery, couldn't get out, and lost almost 5,300 men in a shooting gallery. Grant had finally had enough of this Burnside dude and sent him on a forced leave of absence. After the war Burnside would serve as three-time governor (and later senator) of Rhode Island, mediate peace in the Franco-Prussian War, and serve as the first president of the National Rifle Association.

President Grant

Even though his only professed political aspiration was to become mayor of his hometown so that he could fix the sidewalk outside of his house, Grant's popularity ended up getting him elected to two terms as president of the United States. A lax administrator, he let Congress do pretty much everything while he was in office and isn't really remembered as a great president or anything. After he retired he lost all his money on bad investments, but his memoirs, which he finished just two weeks before his death from throat cancer, were an immediate bestseller that restored his family fortune. Nowadays he's featured on the fifty-dollar bill, which is kind of funny considering that he was almost always broke.

Presidential Soldiers

Including Grant, seven presidents had military service during the Civil War, all of them with the Union. Andrew Johnson was a brigadier general and served as the Union military governor of his home state of Tennessee during the war. Rutherford B. Hayes was part of the force that captured John Hunt Morgan in Ohio and was promoted for bravery during the Battle of Cedar Creek. James A. Garfield fought at Shiloh and was with George Henry Thomas at Chickamauga. Chester A. Arthur was quartermaster-general of the New York militia. Grover Cleveland paid a Polish dude three hundred dollars to take his place in battle, but Benjamin Harrison was a colonel under Sherman during the Atlanta Campaign. The last Civil War vet to become president was William McKinley, an Ohio lieutenant who volunteered as a teenager and drove a wagon of food supplies at the Battle of Antietam.

Arlington National Cemetery

Since that whole "forest full of skulls and bones" thing was totally creepy and all, Grant ordered construction of a major cemetery to bury the remains of Union troops killed at the Battle of the Wilderness. He ended up creating the most famous cemetery in America—Arlington National Cemetery—awesomely setting it up out of spite in the front yard of the house that was owned by Robert E. Lee. The grounds now hold the remains of thousands of American military personnel, 367 Medal of Honor recipients, two presidents, four Kennedys, and the Tomb of the Unknown Soldier.

The Battle of
Spotsylvania Court House

Troops

Union: 100,000

Confederate: 52,000

Casualties

Union: 18,000

Confederate: 12,000

Result

Confederate Victory

Mobile Bay

The US Navy on the Attack

Mobile, Alabama ✳ August 5, 1864

NO MAN EXEMPLIFIED EVERYTHING THE US Navy stood for quite like David Glasgow Farragut. The first man ever appointed to the rank of admiral in US Navy history, Farragut was a hardened veteran of nearly five decades of warfare who never blinked in the face of extreme danger, steamed all-ahead full into combat with every cannon on his warship blazing, and was so mercilessly old-school that even in the new age of armored, ironclad, cannonproof warships he still commanded his fleet from the deck of a three-masted wooden battleship that, in all honesty, wasn't terribly different from the sort of thing Horatio Nelson or Blackbeard the pirate would have taken into combat against their foes on the high seas.

Born in Tennessee in 1801, Farragut had been serving on warships since roughly the time he learned to walk. At the age of nine—a time most kids are thinking about third grade and trying not to pee the bed—this guy was serving as a midshipman on a US Navy warship. At eleven he was loading cannons in combat against the British during the War of 1812. At age twelve he became the youngest captain in US history to command a warship when his commanding officer put him in charge of a Brit vessel that had just surrendered to the States. A year after that, the roles reversed, and after Farragut's ship was taken by a boarding party of Royal Marines he had to spend a few months as a prisoner of war in the dank brig of a Royal Navy vessel. By the time the Civil War rolled around, he was already a forty-nine-year veteran of three wars who was so firmly entrenched in US Navy lore that he didn't even consider the possibility of helping out these whippersnapper Rebels with their uppity rebellion and all that nonsense.

Farragut first gained fame in 1862 when he launched a daring night attack against the critical Confederate port city of New Orleans that was, by most accounts, a suicide charge that somehow ended up working out beautifully. Commanding just twenty-five wooden warships and nineteen tiny mortar schooners, Farragut ignored explicit orders *not* to assault the city, steamed full speed ahead, broke through a Rebel gauntlet consisting of two forts boasting eighty antiship cannons, a wall of floating wooden barricades, three ironclad warships, twelve wooden gunboats, and a dozen or so fireships, somehow capturing the mouth of the Mississippi River and spending the night partying in the French Quarter after losing just one ship under his command.

But now Farragut, the man with so much iron in his guts that he didn't even need to plate his flagship with it, had a more daunting task ahead of him. There was one—only one—Southern port still defying the otherwise unbeatable Federal blockade of the Confederacy: Mobile, Alabama, the most well-defended position on the Confederate coastline.

The "Queen of the Gulf," Mobile was the final base used by Rebel blockade runners. Tens of thousands of barrels of cotton would be shipped to Mobile by rail, then the fastest ships the South could muster would rush these supplies out, slip past the Union blockade, and take their cargo to Europe, where they'd trade it for guns, ammunition, and medical supplies that would then be snuck back into Mobile Bay and distributed by rail to front-line Confederate forces.

Farragut intended to put an end to that noise, cut off the South's last connection with European supplies, and deal the Rebellion a final knockout punch that would finish it once and for all.

The Rebels weren't about to make that easy for him.

Defending the three-mile passage into Mobile Bay were three huge forts—Gaines and Powell in the west and Fort Morgan in the east. Morgan, the most imposing of all of them, was a five-sided stone structure bristling with forty-six cannons capable of erupting most wooden warships into fiery splinters. This searchlight-equipped fortress presided ominously over the only deep-water approach into Mobile Bay—a two-thousand-yard strip of water packed full of deadly floating antiship mines. If Farragut somehow miraculously managed to make it past these three forts and the minefield, he then had to deal with Mobile's defense fleet, a squadron of wooden gunboats led by the Confederate ironclad *Tennessee*, the most powerful iron ship ever built by the Rebel navy. Their other ironclad, CSS *Nashville*, an iron behemoth known as the Monster, was in dry dock for repairs, but for all Farragut knew, that thing could be fully operational in a pinch as well.

David Glasgow Farragut planned to attack with eighteen ships, all but four of which were made of wood. And his battle plan basically amounted to running his fleet right at the enemy and daring them to stop him.

The assault commenced at dawn on August 5, 1864. Farragut deployed his ships in two parallel columns, with his four Monitor-class ironclads (essentially, exact copies of the USS *Monitor* from Hampton Roads) closest to the fort's guns to serve as a shield between the fort's guns and his wooden warships.

At seven AM, these two columns charged out of the morning

fog off the Alabama coast, blitzing into the minefield-studded heart of the Confederacy. All three forts opened fire immediately, ripping apart the quiet scene as the thunderous roar of Fort Morgan's 104-caliber naval artillery shredded the sky with cannon shells that measured almost a foot in diameter. This barrage was supported by long-range cannon blasts from the CSS *Tennessee* and three other Rebel gunboats that were chilling in the safety of the bay behind all the aquatic mines, as everything with a Rebel flag on it attempted to put a wrathful hurting on this column of Federal warships that was bearing down on them as fast as it could sail.

Charging toward the mines, Farragut and his fleet took a pounding, explosions ripping through their sails and smokestacks, filleting gigantic burning chunks out of the hulls of wooden ships, destroying rigging, and exploding crew members all over the decks. Veering away from this horrific wall of death, the lead Monitor, the USS *Tecumseh*, swerved into the Confederate minefield, struck a type of floating wood-enclosed explosive mine known during the Civil War as a torpedo, and had a gigantic gaping hole blown out from her belly below the waterline. With water rushing into what was becoming an inescapable iron coffin, the *Tecumseh* lurched and tipped over on her side, belching black smoke before slipping below the waves and taking ninety-one of her 114-man crew with her.

Looking out at the devastation, seeing the presumably invincible Monitor-class ironclad disappearing beneath the waves, and with fires, shrapnel, and explosions already ravaging his ship, the captain of the lead wooden warship, the USS *Brooklyn*, started to lose his nerve. He slowed his ship, realized how far his column still needed to travel before it reached the relative safety of Mobile Bay (where it then had to deal with the Confederate navy), and started to appreciate how truly borderline reckless this operation really was.

Admiral David Farragut, sixty-three years old, climbed up the mast of his flagship, the USS *Hartford*, to get a better look at the battle. With shrapnel, musket fire, and cannon explosions tearing the rigging around him, Farragut took a piece of rope and lashed himself to the mast so he wouldn't fall, and once he saw the *Brooklyn* slowing down, he bellowed down to his first mate, "I will take the lead!" When his first mate was like, uh, boss, we're kind of getting pounded by artillery and a bunch of torpedo mines just sank one of our toughest ironclad warships, Farragut replied, "Damn the torpedoes, full speed ahead, Drayton! Hard a-starboard!"

With that, the USS *Hartford* swung out of the column, went straight into the middle of the minefield, leapfrogged to the front of the line, and charged right into a hail of bullets, leading Farragut's men from the front of the column without any regard for its own safety.

Everyone got pumped. They charged ahead, undeterred by the tornado of shrapnel, ignoring the sea of explosives capable of ripping their ships into driftwood.

Amazingly, the entire column navigated the minefield without losing another ship. Whether this was skill, luck, terrible mine-laying technology, or some combination of the three has never adequately been proven.

The entire column, led by Farragut, poured into Mobile Bay, uncoupled their ships, and fanned out in attack formation. The wooden ships, far faster than the clunky Monitors, took the lead.

The CSS *Tennessee* was waiting for them with three other gunboats. The *Tennessee*'s commander, Admiral Franklin Buchanan—the Marylander who, incidentally, had commanded the *Merrimack* at the Battle of Hampton Roads—was utterly undeterred by the fact that his lone ironclad was now facing fourteen wooden warships and three exact copies of the ship that had fought his *Merrimack* to a draw back in chapter two. He sneered, lowered the ram, and ordered a full attack on virtually the entire US Navy.

His first target was Farragut's *Hartford*, but the US admiral swerved out of the way at the last second and responded with a close-in broadside that bounced right off the *Tennessee*'s six-inch iron armor. Farragut was then assaulted by the three Confederate wooden gunboats, but he loved every second of it—first he shish-kebabed the CSS *Gaines* into shrapnel with a murderous broadside, and a second volley drove off the CSS *Morgan*, which bolted out of the harbor. The *Hartford* took a severe hit from the third gunboat, the CSS *Selma*, but was able to get the resulting fires under control and keep on trucking.

The *Tennessee*, refusing to give up the fight, struck out from all sides with her complement of turret-mounted cannons, relying on her bulletproof armor to keep her in fighting shape. Unable to punch through her metal plating, Farragut, in yet another act of ironclad bravery, intentionally rammed his shot-to-pieces, partially burning wooden ship into the Confederate ironclad in a futile attempt to disable it.

For the next hour or so, the *Tennessee* and the *Selma* battled the Union assault squadron, but once the Federal Monitor-class gunboats entered the fray it was all but over. The *Selma* was disabled and captured, and danger-close volleys from the turret guns of the US Monitors sheared away enough of the *Tennessee*'s armor to expose her core, smash her steering mechanism, and set fire to her smokestack. Injured by a chunk of shrapnel to the leg and with his ship now virtually dead in the water, Admiral Buchanan finally struck his colors and surrendered. The Gulf of Mexico was now closed to Confederate naval traffic. If the South wanted to continue fighting, it would have to do it without any outside help whatsoever.

Battle of Mobile Bay

Sailors

Union: 5,500

Confederate: 1,500

Casualties

Union: 328

Confederate: 35, plus 1,587 captured

Result

Union Victory

The CSS *Hunley*

Desperate to find a way to break the blockade, the Confederate navy designed, constructed, and operated the first submarine to ever sink an enemy vessel—the CSS *H.L. Hunley.*

A weird-looking, oval-shaped craft, the *Hunley* was thirty feet long, just five feet high, and four feet wide, and somehow accommodated a crew of eight guys who drove the thing by turning a bunch of hand cranks. As far as submarines go, it wasn't exactly the safest thing in the world—during testing, the ship sank twice and about seventeen members of her crew died from various horrible things ranging from fires to drowning. When Horace L. Hunley, the man who financed the project and attached his name to it, was like, "Oh, come on, you wimps, this thing isn't so bad," and led another test run, the ship sank a third time, killing all eight people inside, including Hunley himself.

Nevertheless the Confederates pressed on with the project, somehow convincing eight new guys to test this thing out in a live-fire exercise. The *Hunley*, now known as "the self-propelled coffin," set sail on February 17, 1864, in an attempt to attack the Union ships blockading the port of Charleston, South Carolina. Armed only with a long stick that had a bomb attached to the end of it, the *Hunley* quietly floated toward the USS *Housatonic* and extended her bomb-stick at the enemy. The *Housatonic*, not expecting to be attacked from below, had a hole blown open in her stern and sank to the bottom of the sea, taking five of her crew with her.

The *Hunley* did what the *Hunley* did best—she sank. The shock waves from the explosion shook a hole in her hull, sending her to the bottom of the sea once again.

By the time the wreck of the *Hunley* was finally located in April 1995, the US Navy had more than seventy submarines actively patrolling beneath the waves in seas across the globe. The eight *Hunley* crew members, finally removed from their watery tomb, were buried in Charleston with full military honors in 2004.

The Election of 1864

The American Public Decides the Fate of the War

November 8, 1864 ✷ Washington, DC

> This morning, as for some days past, it seems exceedingly probable that this Administration will not be re-elected. Then it will be my duty to so cooperate with the President-elect as to save the Union between the Election and inauguration; as he will have secured his election on such ground that he cannot possibly save it otherwise.
>
> —Abraham Lincoln

JUST BECAUSE HIS BIRTHDAY IS NOW A NATIONAL holiday, his awesomely bearded mug is carved into the side of a mountain in South Dakota and appears on a good chunk of American currency, and he's routinely voted "world's greatest American" by every popular magazine not printed in South Carolina doesn't necessarily mean that everything was coming up unicorns, rainbows, and smiley-face sunshine happiness roses of joy during the presidency of Abraham Lincoln. The sixteenth president of the United States of America was pressed as hard as any leader of America has ever been, and not just because this dude was fighting a divisive war against half of the states he was supposed to be president of—he was also constantly being hassled not only by war-weary domestic enemies in the North but also by members of his own political party, to the point where he was actually very close to not *even being nominated as the Republican candidate for president in the election of 1864.*

Give that a second to sink in the next time you whip out a five-dollar bill to pay for an Extra Value Meal.

Born in poverty in a log cabin in rural Kentucky, Abraham Lincoln didn't have the typical background of a US president. He'd worked as a ditchdigger and then a shop owner, and loved watching wrestling and bare-knuckled boxing matches. Coming from basically nothing, Lincoln worked his way up, got elected to the Illinois Legislature at age twenty-three, became a successful lawyer, won the presidency despite not appearing on the ballot in half the states of the Union, refused to back down when challenged head-on by the Rebellion, and then proceeded to lead his beloved country charging into the war that would define his entire presidency.

Despite his unstoppable tenacity and American Dream–style rise to power in the North, Lincoln's popularity still changed with the tide of his war. And sure, for the most part by the middle of 1864 there was a lot to be happy about—the Rebel armies had been gobsmacked at Chattanooga and Gettysburg, the Union navy controlled the Mississippi and maintained a mostly inescapable blockade on the Confederate coast, and Federal armies were on the march in Virginia and Tennessee. Of course, on the other hand, U. S. Grant couldn't move his army fifteen feet without getting a thousand Union soldiers shot to death, and by summer he was spending more time digging holes outside Petersburg than he was punching Robert E. Lee in the junk. The end of the war was still a long way off, and, even if it did mean a Union victory, would it be worth the human sacrifice and loss? Wouldn't it just be easier to let the Confederates have their own stupid country and call it a day anyway?

These were the questions going into the presidential election of 1864—the single most important election in American history and the first democratic election in history to ever be held in a country that was currently going through a civil war. It would be, at its core, a referendum on whether or not the American public wanted to continue fighting the Civil War.

Lincoln's political opponents had a hardcore beef with the chief executive. For starters, not only was Lincoln taxing the pants off the population to pay for an ultra-expensive, incredibly bloody war against a hostile country that didn't want to be reintegrated into the Union (no bigs), but he also instituted the first national draft, basically forcing every able-bodied

American man between the ages of eighteen and thirty-five to charge headlong into Confederate artillery. He'd made a primary goal of the war to emancipate a population that, quite honestly, a lot of poor Northern industrial workers didn't really care about emancipating. Meanwhile, Lincoln was also trampling on American civil liberties, first by shutting down any newspaper that disagreed with him, and second by suspending the writ of *habeas corpus*, meaning that if you went out in public and said, hey, maybe this war thing isn't such a good idea after all, pre-NSA Federal agents could show up at your house, arrest you without cause, and hold you in prison indefinitely without a trial. Plus, south of the border, French emperor Napoleon III had set up a French-controlled puppet government in Mexico, and Lincoln was utterly powerless to do anything about a European-style monarchy being established next door to the United States because he was kind of busy with the whole Civil War thing.

So, in 1864, the Democrats put out the man they thought should be the next president of the United States of America—our good buddy General George B. McClellan. That's right, the same General George B. McClellan who couldn't win the Battle of Antietam even though he was *looking at the enemy's plan of attack*. McClellan, who is now famous for being a military commander who never actually wanted to fight anyone, ran on the platform that the war could be brought to an end peacefully, without emancipation of the slaves, and that the

United States should end the war at all costs even if it meant letting the South ride off into the sunset and do its own thing.

Lincoln, meanwhile, almost didn't even win the Republican Party nomination for president in 1864. No president had been nominated for a second term since 1840, let alone reelected, and there was a huge split among the Republicans between people who thought Lincoln was cool and people who thought he wasn't enough of a jerk to the Confederates. So the Radical Republican branch of his party put up a guy named John C. Frémont to oppose him. Frémont was a Mexican-American War vet and mountain man adventurer who had mapped the Oregon Trail and Sierra Nevada Mountains, discovered Lake Tahoe and Mount St. Helens, and once saved famous explorer Kit Carson's life by trampling a would-be assailant with his horse. Lincoln tried to appease the Republicans by dropping his vice president, Hannibal Hamlin, for a guy named Andrew Johnson (who would end up being pretty important someday), but just two weeks before the election Frémont was still on the ballot as a second Republican candidate.

As the polls continued looking worse and worse, Lincoln became more and more convinced that defeat in the election—and by extension the war—would be increasingly likely. Still, he stayed strong in the belief that he was doing the best thing for his country, and pressed on without changing his policy or his "let's get these jerks" aggressiveness in conducting the war. He wasn't a guy who was about to give up and run home to Mama just because a few people came out and said they didn't like his attitude or whatever. He knew the election would hinge on the fate of the war, and by 1864 he'd finally found the man who could get the job done right: Major General William Tecumseh Sherman.

"Uncle Billy" Sherman is, to this day, the single most hated man south of the Mason-Dixon Line. One of the roughest warriors the United States of America has ever produced, Sherman's name is tantamount to profanity in Georgia, stories of his campaigns are told around South Carolina campfires as ghost stories, and his imposing facial hair continues to send chills down the spines of Southerners 150 years later.

Born in Lancaster, Ohio, in 1820, this intimidating career soldier was orphaned at age nine, pulled himself up by the bootstraps, received appointment to the United States Military Academy at West Point, fought in the Seminole Wars and Mexican-American War, then eventually became the superintendent of the military school that became Louisiana State University. An ardent supporter of all things red, white, and blue, Sherman angrily resigned his professorship when Louisiana seceded and immediately offered his sword to the service of the United States. He commanded a brigade at the First Bull Run, led a division at Shiloh, oversaw an assault against Vicksburg, commanded a wing of the army at Chattanooga, and was once relieved of duty for having a nervous breakdown. Sherman was reinstated by fellow Ohioan and close friend Ulysses S. Grant (Sherman would later say, "He stood by me when I was crazy and I stood by him when he was drunk"), who correctly realized that this dude was exactly the sort of warmongering human buzz saw you wanted to have at the head of a campaigning army. When Grant went east to deal with Lee, he wisely put Sherman in charge of the US Army west of the Mississippi. Sherman responded by undertaking one of the most infamous campaigns in American history, changing the face of warfare in the process and almost single-handedly generating enough military victories to have every newspaper in North America printing hand-drawn pictures of Abraham Lincoln high-fiving the Statue of Liberty while bald eagles weep beautiful tears of joy. (This would have been super-extra-impressive because the Statue of Liberty hadn't ever been created yet.)

On May 7, 1864, Sherman departed his base of operations in Chattanooga at the head of one hundred thousand dedicated, well-armed soldiers, his sights set on one thing and one thing alone—the capture and utter destruction of Atlanta, Georgia. He intended to march his armies one hundred miles into the Confederate heartland, destroy Rebel forces with extreme prejudice wherever they opposed him, then turn east and cut a swath of destruction through Georgia that would inspire his fellow Northerners, cripple the Rebel economy, and break the Southern people of any desire to continue fighting this war.

Standing against Sherman's legions was Confederate

general Joseph E. Johnston, at the head of an exhausted, demoralized, undersupplied force of just sixty-two thousand men. Brought in to replace ultra-terrible Braxton Bragg, Johnston knew he didn't have the manpower to attack Sherman head-on, so he adopted the same strategy that got him fired as commander of the Army of Northern Virginia a few years back: Fight a defensive war, hold the line, and get out of there if it looks like you're going to take major losses. When he received word of the Union advance, Johnston ordered his men to dig trenches, sight their guns, and prepare to fight off wave after wave of Union soldiers.

This was a pretty sound plan, except for the fact that William Tecumseh Sherman had absolutely no intention of stupidly hurling his men into the meat grinder in a series of idiotic frontal assaults. One of the first Union commanders to understand that the entire warfare had changed, Sherman continually refused to recklessly rush face-first into Confederate artillery like his predecessors. Instead, he wisely used his numbers to his advantage, circled around the enemy, and tried to swamp the Confederates.

At Resaca, Rome, New Hope Church, Dallas, Altoona Pass, and a half-dozen other places, Johnston found himself outmaneuvered and outmatched, and wisely retreated. This wasn't a beautiful, glamorous campaign full of daring bayonet charges, heroic last stands, and incredible feats of human endurance braving storms of bullets in a glorious display of

sword-swinging mayhem aimed at nobly reunifying this country under the Stars and Stripes. It was a smart, competent, efficient, and unblockable series of one-two combination punches
that wore the Rebels down, calmly battered at their defenses,
and achieved an unprecedented victory thanks to sheer grit,
determination, and cold, calculating devastation. There's a
reason they named a World War II tank after Sherman.

Rebel president Jefferson Davis, who never liked Johnston
much to begin with, sent the general packing and replaced
him with a man who had a well-deserved reputation for ultra-
aggressive behavior that was somewhere between "utter fearlessness" and "reckless insanity" on the military command
spectrum—John Bell Hood, the hard-fighting Kentuckian
who had personally led dozens of brazen charges at fortified
enemy positions on battlefields from Antietam to Chickamauga. The ultimate shock troop commander, Hood had lost
an arm at Gettysburg and a leg at Chickamauga, but he still
got out there, strapped himself into his saddle so he could lead
from the front, and told his men that they were going to take
the fight to the enemy with, you guessed it, a series of idiotic
charges straight on into the teeth of the enemy lines.

By the time the smoke cleared, the Rebels had buried
fifteen thousand men in under a week. Sherman encircled
Atlanta, bombarded it with artillery, cut off its railroad access,
and demanded complete, unconditional surrender. Unable to
hold, Hood withdrew from the city.

On September 2, 1864—two months before the presidential election—General William Tecumseh Sherman marched
the victorious Union army into Atlanta, the economic capital of the Confederacy. To celebrate, he gave the residents of
the city twenty-four hours to evacuate their homes before he
torched the city to the ground.

John Frémont withdrew from the race a week or two later.
McClellan popped a few antacids and wiped a little sweat off
his brow.

November 8, 1864, was a gray, cold, rainy day that would

decide whether the Union would continue the war or seek peace with the Rebellion. When the final returns were in, McClellan had received 1.8 million votes to Lincoln's 2.2 million. The president had won reelection by just three hundred thousand votes, carrying both New York and Pennsylvania by less than eighteen thousand votes each.

Most tellingly, Lincoln had received over 70 percent of the soldiers' votes. These men knew they were voting to go to war and potentially their own deaths, but they weren't about to let their comrades' sacrifices be in vain.

They were going to finish what they'd started three years earlier.

They were going to keep fighting until this war was won.

I earnestly believe that the consequences of this day's work...will be to the lasting advantage, if not the very salvation, of this country. I am thankful to God for this approval of the people.

—Abraham Lincoln, 1864

Sherman's Legacy

When Grant became president in 1869, he appointed Sherman to the post of commanding general of the US Army, a post Sherman held for the next fifteen years. Under his watch, the United States fought several wars against the Plains Indians, most notably the Sioux. When Sherman died in 1891, an old adversary, eighty-four-year-old former Confederate general Joseph E. Johnston, was the lead pallbearer.

Jefferson Davis

Lincoln's counterpart, Confederate president Jefferson Davis, never really worried too much about elections, mostly because he never held any. Davis, who was born a few counties away from Lincoln in Kentucky but grew up in Mississippi, was a Mexican-American War hero, a seasoned US senator, and one of the foremost champions of the states' rights to make their own rules instead of being told what to do by the Federal government. Davis was the man who gave the order to fire on Fort Sumter to start the Civil War, but the job of creating a new government in the middle of a war for survival was no small feat, and many bitter historians like to argue that this guy was the reason the South didn't win the war. He probably wasn't.

The Atlanta Campaign

Troops
Union: 100,000
Confederate: 60,000

Casualties
Union: 31,687
Confederate: 34,979

Result
Union Victory

Sherman's March

My aim then was to whip the rebels, to humble their pride, to follow them to their inmost recesses, and make them fear and dread us.

—Major General William Tecumseh Sherman, US Army

From this point on, things get bad for the Confederacy. Like really bad.

After taking Atlanta and destroying the remnants of the

Confederate army in the west, William Tecumseh Sherman, embittered by years of brutal conflict with the Rebels, set out from Atlanta with sixty thousand men and one mission—"make Georgia howl."

Organizing two columns covering a forty- to sixty-mile-wide arc, Sherman initiated a scorched-earth policy that we know today as "total war." Basically, his army marched from Atlanta to Savannah without supply or communications lines, living off the land on crops and food they foraged from farms along the way and utterly destroying anything the Rebels had that could have helped them fight the war. Facing a paltry thirteen thousand Confederate soldiers—mostly inexperienced local militia armed with ancient weaponry—Sherman's men vanquished enemy fighters, devastated farms and industries, ripped up rail lines, knocked down fence posts, freed slaves, and spent five weeks wreaking an estimated eighty million dollars' worth of damage across a 285-mile-long swath of the Confederate heartland. Issuing an order for his men to refrain from looting, pillaging, and harming local populations, Sherman didn't hesitate to supply his troops with captured food, famously declaring to his subordinates, "Let it be known that if a farmer wishes to burn his cotton, his house, his family, and himself, he may do so. But not his corn. We want that."

By December, Sherman's columns had reached the Atlantic coast, surrounding the last ten thousand Rebel soldiers inside the walls of Savannah, Georgia. Rather than launching a full-scale assault, Sherman simply sent the garrison's commander a letter ordering him to leave town or face the "harshest measures." The Rebel commander didn't stick around to figure out what Sherman meant by that.

The next day, Sherman was sending a telegram to Washington, DC, offering President Lincoln a "Christmas present"—one hundred fifty cannons, twenty-five thousand bales of cotton, and the utter submission of Georgia.

Lincoln ordered him to turn north, keep up the good work, and not stop marching until he'd linked his army up with Grant's and set the stage for a final showdown with Robert E. Lee.

Sherman's response? "The truth is the whole army is burning with an insatiable desire to wreak vengeance upon South Carolina. I almost tremble at her fate."

Major General William Tecumseh Sherman

The End of the Line

The Battle of Sayler's Creek

Rice, Virginia ✳ *April 6, 1865*

> My God, has the army dissolved?
>
> —Robert E. Lee

BACK IN PETERSBURG, VIRGINIA, THINGS WERE looking bad for Robert E. Lee and the once-invincible Army of Northern Virginia.

By the spring of 1865, nine months of grinding trench warfare had taken their toll on the Southern forces. Now, with his men starving from a severe shortage of food and almost completely surrounded by Grant's army, and with reports of a victorious, fearsome horde of Union troops under the command of William Tecumseh Sherman rampaging their way north through the Carolinas toward Petersburg, Lee knew his options were grim: Surrender, escape, or fight to the death in an unwinnable last stand against impossible odds.

The final straw came when Grant's brilliant cavalry commander Philip Sheridan—a short little dude with a mustache, who was almost as proficient at fighting as he was at swearing—cut off the last rail line to Richmond by personally leading his cavalry in a massive charge at the Battle of Five Forks. With his defenses crumbling, Lee knew he had to act.

Unwilling to give up, Lee opted for one desperate, last-ditch effort—on the night of April 2, 1865, he led the Army of Northern Virginia out of Petersburg, abandoning the Confederate capital of Richmond to the enemy. His plan was to make a break for Amelia Courthouse, a storehouse a few miles west, where he was expecting a large shipment of food to be waiting for him. From there, he would lead his forces south into North Carolina, link up with the army of Joseph E. Johnston that was still futilely attempting to oppose Sherman, and then the combined military of the Confederate States would attempt to first beat Sherman, then head north and beat Grant. It was a bold plan, unlikely to succeed but not *completely* impossible.

Lee had a head start, because he knew Grant had to stop and occupy Richmond. Unfortunately, when Lee reached Amelia Courthouse, he found it stocked with bullets and cannonballs—not food. Even worse, the road south into North Carolina had already been cut off by Sheridan's fast-moving cavalrymen, dispatched by Grant specifically for the purpose of harassing Lee's retreating army.

So, reluctantly, Lee ordered his forces to make a break sixty miles west for Appomattox Courthouse, where a stockpile of rations was waiting for them.

The Army of Northern Virginia, divided into four corps, began moving as quickly as possible toward Appomattox. Sheridan eagerly pursued the fleeing enemy forces, harassing the Rebels every single step of the way.

His tenacity paid off. Ewell's and Anderson's corps, the two forces responsible for guarding the Army of Northern Virginia's two hundred ammunition and ambulance wagons, had been taking the brunt of the Federals' irritating raids, and as they neared the bridge over Sayler's Creek in Rice, Virginia, they stopped to form a line and counterattack Sheridan's troops. Unfortunately, the rest of the Confederate forces didn't know these two units had halted, and within a few hours there was a two-mile-wide gap between these two corps, the Confederate baggage train, and the rest of the Rebel army.

Into that gap rode the Union army's most flamboyant cavalry commander—George Armstrong Custer.

Custer, a loud, flashy, fiery, relentlessly self-promoting warrior who strongly believed there wasn't a situation on earth that couldn't be solved with a spirited saber charge from Union cavalry and a six-shooter to the chest, was one of the Federal army's

most successful cavalrymen. Finishing last in his class at West
Point thanks to excessive demerits and a healthy disrespect for
authority, Custer still managed to get himself a commission, and
was fighting on the battlefields of First Manassas two months
after his graduation. He'd go on to personally lead dozens of
cavalry charges at the head of his men, having eleven horses
shot out from under him while capturing 111 artillery pieces,
sixty-five battle flags, and ten thousand prisoners during the
Civil War without losing a single gun or flag.

Acting fast, Custer had now positioned his Michigan
Cavalry Division (known as Custer's Wolverines) in the
perfect position to encircle and cut the Army of Northern
Virginia in half with one fell swoop. When Rebel forces
moved to reopen the lines, he personally led a stampeding
cavalry charge that overran their position and captured
several pieces of artillery, pinning Anderson's corps in place
and holding them there long enough for Union infantry to
arrive on the scene.

Ewell and Anderson were trapped. Every man there knew
this would be their last stand.

Ewell's Reserve Corps was dug in on a ridge with 3,700
men, staring down at seven thousand men from General Horatio Wright's Union VI Corps. Ewell, whose forces consisted
mostly of Richmond garrison units, heavy artillerymen, navy
sailors, and prison guards who were seeing some of their first
action of the war, took cover behind their hastily built defenses

as Wright, the Connecticut-born US Army engineer who would later oversee the construction of the Brooklyn Bridge and the Washington Monument, ordered up his artillery. Ewell had no cannons in his command to reply to the half-hour barrage that followed, as twenty Union artillery guns rained death down on his position. After thirty minutes of cannon fire, Wright ordered his men to advance up the hill.

Seven thousand Union troops advanced toward 3,700 Confederates. The Rebels held their fire. As the Union got close, the soldiers in the front rank waved white handkerchiefs, taunting the Confederates to surrender. Ewell's corps responded with a volley, leveled at the knees and legs of the Union lines from one hundred yards out. The volley mowed down many men in the first rank, but the Union attack relentlessly continued. A second volley staggered the advance once more and, seeing an advantage, some Rebel commanders ordered their men to fix bayonets and stand fast against the wall of blue jackets now facing them.

First among them was the heavy artillery, led by a one-legged man ironically named Crutchfield who'd had his leg blown off at Chancellorsville. According to one major who somehow survived the swirling fray, "Quicker than I can tell it the battle denigrated into butchery and a confused melee of brutal personal conflicts...men kill each other with bayonets and the butts of muskets, and even bite each other's throats and ears and noses, rolling on the ground like wild beasts."

Outnumbered, battered on all sides, and taking double-canister shot from Union artillery pieces, the Rebel assault staggered. When the Union VI Corps emerged from the fray victorious, the surviving members of Ewell's forces began surrendering rather than experience their wrath.

A few hundred yards to the southwest, Anderson's corps wasn't faring much better. He attempted to break out, but was thrown back by Custer's and Sheridan's troopers with their repeating rifles. Seeing an opportunity to lead one final attack to break the backs of his hated enemies, the brazen Custer unsheathed his saber, rode to the front of his troops, and ordered a charge at the gallop right at Anderson's left flank. With a cheer so loud it drowned out the sound of the bugle calls, Custer's Wolverines wheeled into line and spurred their horses to the gallop, slamming into the starving, demoralized Confederates, the Michiganders seemingly unfazed by staring down the barrels of hundreds of muskets and cannons.

Among this charge was Custer's younger brother, Captain Thomas Ward Custer of the Sixth Michigan Cavalry. Enlisting at sixteen after lying to his recruiting officer, Tom Custer had served at Chickamauga and Atlanta with the Twenty-First Ohio Infantry, and had been a company commander in Custer's division since the Union attack on Richmond had begun. An ultra-fearless warrior, just three days earlier he'd rode his horse across enemy lines and captured the battle flag of the

Second North Carolina—an act that earned him the Medal of Honor. Now he saw his opportunity to repeat this action.

Custer's men bore down on the Rebel forces, who were firing from behind the cover of a wooden stockade they'd built from ripped-up fences. Ignoring the incoming fire, Tom Custer galloped ahead, drawing double pistols and jumping his horse over the barricade straight into the middle of the Rebel positions, firing his revolvers left and right at anything he could see. His men followed with him, plowing into the Rebel lines and scattering them with intense close-range fire.

Except Tom Custer wasn't done yet. As his men were carrying the Confederate position, he noticed a color sergeant attempting to rally Rebel forces behind a second line of prepared defenses. The sergeant was shouting for his men and

waving the Confederate "Stars and Bars" flag for all it was worth, raging against the impending death of his beloved Confederacy. Custer, seeing this, charged his horse ahead once more, leaving behind his men in their melee and bearing down hard on the flag bearer. The sergeant, seeing a battle-raging Yankee dual-wielding revolvers stampeding in his direction, pulled his pistol and unloaded it at extreme close range, shooting Tom Custer in the face, blowing a hole in his cheek that immediately started gushing massive amounts of blood. Custer, completely undeterred, grabbed the sergeant's flag with one hand and shot him in the heart with his other, killing the sergeant instantly.

Triumphantly waving the captured Rebel battle flag, Tom Custer rode back to his brother, handed it off, and proceeded to go back into the fray. George Armstrong Custer tried to persuade him to get medical attention immediately, and when Tom refused, Armstrong placed him under arrest and had two orderlies drag him to the hospital tent.

Tom would survive the battle and receive a second Medal of Honor. He would be the first American soldier to receive two Medals of Honor, the only man to receive two in the Civil War, and presumably the only person to earn two Medals of Honor in the span of *three days*.

Their flank turned, Anderson's troops broke. Some ran for it and escaped to Farmville to link up with the rest of Lee's forces, but most were ridden down and captured, and the baggage train was seized by troops from Union II Corps.

April 6, 1865, known as "Black Thursday" by the Confederates, would be the last major battle fought by the Army of Northern Virginia. Seventy-seven hundred Rebel soldiers were captured—a quarter of Lee's army—along with three hundred wagons, sixteen cannons, and dozens of battle flags and regimental colors. Among the prisoners were six generals, including Richard Ewell and George Washington Custis Lee, Robert E. Lee's oldest son. It would be the largest number of prisoners ever taken in a battle in North America. The Federals suffered 1,180 casualties.

Reduced to just twenty-eight thousand starving, demoralized men under his command, Lee continued his race toward Appomattox, but on the night of April 8, just a day's ride away, he scouted ahead and saw the road to Appomattox lined with campfires of Union forces. He was too late. Appomattox, and its store of food, was already gone.

The following day, April 9, 1865, Robert E. Lee met with Ulysses S. Grant to discuss terms of surrender. Grant offered him peaceful terms—men could keep their swords and their horses and would be pardoned and paroled to go free to their homes. Lee, upon leaving the meeting, sorrowfully addressed his troops: "Men, we have fought through the war together. I have done my best for you. My heart is too full to say more."

The American Civil War, for all intents and purposes, was over.

Custer's Last Stand

The table where Lee signed the surrender documents was eventually purchased by General Philip Sheridan, who gave it to George A. Custer's wife as a present. After the war, Custer's legend would continue to grow as he served as a dashing Indian-fighting American hero in command of the famous Seventh US Cavalry Regiment, battling the Sioux across the Great Plains. Despite all of his bravery, his overconfidence would end up being his undoing—on June 25, 1876, he would lead two hundred sixty troopers into a battle against over three thousand Sioux warriors led by their war chief, Crazy Horse. Surrounded on all sides, using their fallen horses for cover, the men of the Seventh, including George and Tom Custer, would be wiped out to the last man.

Final Surrender

The last Confederate general to surrender was also the highest-ranking American Indian soldier on either side—Cherokee warrior Stand Watie. Commander of the Cherokee Mounted Rifles, Brigadier General Stand Watie joined the Confederacy figuring, hey, they probably won't treat the American Indians a whole lot worse than the United States, and he boldly led his unit of warrior braves into battle beginning in August 1861, through his daring charges at Federal infantry in the Battle of Pea Ridge, all the way through his final surrender to overwhelming numbers at Doaksville, in present-day Oklahoma, on June 23, 1865.

Davis Flees

Confederate president Jefferson Davis fled Richmond one day before Lee's army, making a last desperate ride for Texas to keep the Confederacy alive. He was captured on May 10, 1865, near Irwinville, Georgia, by members of the First Wisconsin and Fourth Michigan Cavalry. Davis ended up spending two years in prison in Fort Monroe, Virginia, before being released.

Sayler's Versus Sailor's

Think that whole naming-battles-for-rivers-versus-towns thing is confusing? Try this one on: Both sides agree to calling this one the Battle of Sayler's Creek, but there's no consensus on how exactly to *spell* it. The earliest maps from 1751 spell it *Sailor's*, but the National Park Service calls it *Sayler's*. Other accepted spellings like *Saylor's*, *Sailer's*, and *Saiyloers*, for the record, are always wrong.

The Battle of Sayler's Creek

Troops

Union: 16,000

Confederate: 11,500

Casualties

Union: 1,150

Confederate: 1,130 plus 7,700 captured

Result

Union Victory

Custer ready for his third charge at Sayler's Creek,
April 6. 1865; drawn by Alfred R. Waud on April 6, 1865

General Order No. 9

After four years of arduous service marked by unsurpassed courage and fortitude, the Army of Northern Virginia has been compelled to yield to overwhelming numbers and resources.

I need not tell the survivors of so many hard fought battles, who have remained steadfast to the last, that I have consented to the result from no distrust of them.

But feeling that valour and devotion could accomplish nothing that could compensate for the loss that must have attended the continuance of the contest, I have determined to avoid the useless sacrifice of those whose past services have endeared them to their countrymen.

By the terms of the agreement, officers and men can return to their homes and remain until exchanged. You will take with you the satisfaction that proceeds from the consciousness of duty faithfully performed, and I earnestly pray that a merciful God will extend to you his blessing and protection.

With an unceasing admiration of your constancy and devotion to your Country, and a grateful remembrance of your kind and generous consideration for myself, I bid you an affectionate farewell.

—R. E. Lee, General, General Order No. 9

Conclusion

✪ ✪ ✪

What General Lee's feelings were I do not know. As he was a man of much dignity, with an impassible face, it was impossible to say whether he felt inwardly glad that the end had finally come, or felt sad over the result, and was too manly to show it. Whatever his feelings, they were entirely concealed from my observation; but my own feelings, which had been quite jubilant on the receipt of his letter, were sad and depressed. I felt like anything rather than rejoicing at the downfall of a foe who had fought so long and valiantly, and had suffered so much for a cause, though that cause was, I believe, one of the worst for which a people ever fought, and one for which there was the least excuse. I do not question, however, the sincerity of the great mass of those who were opposed to us.

—*Ulysses S. Grant*

THE CIVIL WAR WAS, BY FAR, THE MOST destructive conflict in American history. At a time when the population of this country was one-tenth what it is today, this war left 750,000 men dead, 476,000 wounded, and 400,000 missing or captured, for a total of nearly 1.5 million casualties—more than the number of US casualties sustained in World War I, World War II, Vietnam, the Revolutionary War, the Spanish-American War, Desert Storm, and the current military operations in Afghanistan and Iraq *combined*.

So what did we learn?

The war was tough on both sides, particularly the South, which sustained the brunt of the action. Reconstruction, the period following the war when Radical Republicans in the North passed laws forcing Southerners to change their ways, was exceptionally hard on the former Confederate states.

In the end, however, this country was better for having gone through this crisis. The amendments that passed following the war—those that freed the slaves and gave voting rights to black American men (women of any ethnicity across America would have to wait another fifty years before gaining the right to vote)—were a shining example of the principles of freedom and liberty the United States was founded on. The two halves of the country, South and North, stayed strong, regrouped, and reunified to make a more powerful, more cohesive nation, building the United States of America up from a regional power in North America to a massive, self-aware industrial powerhouse that would quickly leap to the forefront of world politics for a century and a half to come. It shaped the entire direction that this country took, and in the end, we were stronger and better off for having weathered this potentially disastrous storm successfully.

We also learned that nothing we have is free. That everything we have is because brave men and women paid for it in blood.

Acknowledgments

★ ★ ★

What a cruel thing is war; to separate and destroy families and friends, and mar the purest joys and happiness God has granted us in this world; to fill our hearts with hatred instead of love for our neighbors, and to devastate the fair face of this beautiful world! I pray that, on this day when only peace and good-will are preached to mankind, better thoughts may fill the hearts of our enemies and turn them to peace....My heart bleeds at the death of every one of our gallant men.

—*Robert E. Lee*

THIS BOOK IS FOR MY FATHER, WHO HAS LIVED and breathed the Civil War for over twenty years. I would also like to send my deepest and most sincere thank-you to the following people for helping me in every step of this process:

To my amazing wife, Simone, the most beautiful, most incredible, coolest woman I have ever known. I can't tell you how much I appreciate your endless support throughout the entire process of writing this book. I love you more than anything.

To my mom, and my brothers, Clay and John, for always being available to help me work through tough situations whether they're book-related or not; to my stepdaughter, Presley, for giving me plenty of *Minecraft* breaks exactly when I needed them; and to Brian Snoddy, for grabbing lunch at Yuji's every time I forgot the difference between W. H. Fitzhugh Lee and Regular Fitzhugh Lee and started to wonder what it all means anyway.

To my amazing editor, Connie Hsu, for taking on this project, championing it, brutalizing my manuscript in all the right ways, and always being available to assist me every step of the way, and to her assistant, Leslie Shumate, for taking an extra set of eyes to everything.

To my fact-checker, Allison Jordan of Gettysburg College, for keeping me honest and catching a massive mix-up where I listed Jefferson Davis as being from Missouri instead of Mississippi.

To my agents, Farley Chase of Chase Literary and Sean Daily of Hotchkiss, for always backing me up and for dealing with all the boring business and contract negotiation stuff so I don't have to.

Finally, I would also like to say thank you to all who have served, or currently serve, their country by fighting for what they believe in. Your sacrifice will never go unappreciated.

Bibliography

⭐ ⭐ ⭐

O! had I the ability, and could reach the nation's ear, I would, to-day, pour out a fiery stream of biting ridicule, blasting reproach, withering sarcasm, and stern rebuke. For it is not light that is needed, but fire; it is not the gentle shower, but thunder. We need the storm, the whirlwind, and the earthquake. The feeling of the nation must be quickened; the conscience of the nation must be roused.

—Frederick Douglass

Abbott, Karen. "The Siren of the Shenandoah." *The New York Times* (online). May 23, 2012. opinionator.blogs.nytimes.com/2012/05/23/the-siren-of-the-shenandoah.

Adler, Dennis. *Guns of the Civil War.* Minneapolis: Zenith, 2011.

Alexander, Thomas E., and Dan K. Utley. *Faded Glory: A Century of Forgotten Military Sites, Then and Now.* College Station: Texas A&M University Press, 2012.

Axelrod, Alan. *Generals South, Generals North: The Commanders of the Civil War Reconsidered.* Guilford, CT: Globe Pequot, 2011.

Bales, Kevin. *New Slavery: A Reference Handbook.* 2nd ed. Santa Barbara, CA: ABC-CLIO, 2004.

Ballard, Michael B. *Civil War Mississippi: A Guide.* Jackson: University of Mississippi Press, 2000.

Banasik, Michael E., ed. *Cavaliers of the Brush: Quantrill and His Men.* Iowa City, IA: Camp Pope Bookshop, 2003.

Barney, William L. *The Oxford Encyclopedia of the Civil War*. New York: Oxford University Press, 2011.

Barthel, Thomas. *Abner Doubleday: A Civil War Biography*. Jefferson, NC: McFarland, 2010.

Beattie, Daniel. *Brandy Station 1863: First Step Towards Gettysburg*. Oxford, UK: Osprey, 2008.

Bergeron, Paul H. *Andrew Johnson's Civil War and Reconstruction*. Knoxville: University of Tennessee Press, 2011.

Bilby, Joseph G. *Civil War Firearms: Their Historical Background and Tactical Use*. Cambridge, MA: Da Capo Press, 2005.

Blackford, W. W. *War Years with Jeb Stuart*. South Lancaster, MA: Read Books, 2007.

Blanton, DeAnne, and Lauren M. Cook. *They Fought Like Demons: Women Soldiers in the Civil War*. Reprint, New York: Vintage Books, 2003.

Boatner, Mark Mayo, III. *The Civil War Dictionary* (rev. ed.). New York: McKay, 1988.

Bollett, Alfred J. "The Truth about Civil War Surgery." *Civil War Times* (June 12, 2006). historynet.com/the-truth-about-civil-war-surgery-2.htm.

Boyd, Belle. *Belle Boyd in Camp and Prison*. New York: Blelock, 1865.

Brown, Hallie Quinn. *Homespun Heroines and Other Women of Distinction*. New York: Oxford University Press, 1988.

Carol, Steven S. *Encyclopedia of Days*. Bloomington, IN: iUniverse, 2009.

Castel, Albert E. *Winning and Losing in the Civil War: Essays and Stories*. Columbia: University of South Carolina Press, 1996.

Castel, Albert E., and Thomas Goodrich. *Bloody Bill Anderson: The Short, Savage Life of a Civil War Guerilla*. Mechanicsburg, PA: Stackpole Books, 1998.

Catton, Bruce. *Gettysburg: The Final Fury*. New York: Doubleday, 1990.

Chamberlain, Joshua Lawrence. *The Passing of the Armies: An Account of the Final Campaign of the Army of the Potomac*. Lincoln: University of Nebraska Press, 1998.

Chambers, John Whiteclay, II, and Fred Anderson, eds. *The Oxford Companion to American Military History*. New York: Oxford University Press, 1999.

Christensen, Lawrence O., William E. Foley, Gary R. Kramer, and Kenneth H. Winn, eds. *Dictionary of Missouri Biography*. Columbia: University of Missouri Press, 1999.

The Civil War Trust. "Saving America's Civil War Battlefields." civilwar.org.

Cotham, Edward T., Jr. *Sabine Pass: The Confederacy's Thermopylae*. Austin: University of Texas Press, 2004.

Cross, Robin, and Rosalind Miles. *Warrior Women: 3000 Years of Courage and Heroism*. New York: Metro Books, 2011.

Danson, Edwin. *Drawing the Line: How Mason and Dixon Surveyed the Most*

Famous Border in America. Hoboken, NJ: John Wiley and Sons, 2001.

Davis, Paul K. *100 Decisive Battles: From Ancient Times to the Present.* New York: Oxford University Press, 2001.

Davis, William C., Brian C. Pohanka, and Don Troiani, eds. *Civil War Journal: The Legacies.* Nashville: Thomas Nelson, 1999.

Day, Carl F. *Tom Custer: Ride to Glory.* Norman: University of Oklahoma Press, 2004.

De Pauw, Linda Grant. *Battle Cries and Lullabies: Women in War from Prehistory to the Present.* Norman: University of Oklahoma Press, 1998.

Desjardin, Thomas A. *These Honored Dead: How the Story of Gettysburg Shaped American Memory.* Cambridge, MA: Da Capo Press, 2003.

Douglas, Henry Kyd. *I Rode with Stonewall: The War Experiences of the Youngest Member of Jackson's Staff.* Robinsdale, MN: Fawcett, 1961.

Eggleston, Larry G. *Women in the Civil War: Extraordinary Stories of Soldiers, Spies, Nurses, Doctors, Crusaders, and Others.* Jefferson, NC: McFarland, 2003.

Erwin, James W. *Guerillas in Civil War Missouri.* Charleston, SC: History Press, 2012.

Farwell, Byron. *The Encyclopedia of Nineteenth-Century Land Warfare: An Illustrated World View.* New York: W. W. Norton, 2001.

Faust, Patricia L., ed. *Historical Times Illustrated Encyclopedia of the Civil War.* New York: HarperCollins, 1986.

Fisher, Ernest F., Jr. *Guardians of the Republic: A History of the NonCommissioned Officer Corps of the U.S. Army.* Mechanicsburg, PA: Stackpole Books, 2001.

Flayderman, Norm. *Flayderman's Guide to Antique American Firearms and Their Values.* 9th ed. Iola, WI: Gun Digest Books, 2007.

Foote, Shelby. *The Civil War: A Narrative.* 2nd ed. 3 vols. (Vintage). New York: Random House, 1974.

Fox, Stephen. *Wolf of the Deep: Raphael Semmes and the Notorious Confederate Raider CSS Alabama.* First Vintage Civil War Library Edition. New York: Random House, 2008.

Frank, Lisa Tendrich, ed. *Women in the American Civil War.* 2 vols. Santa Barbara, CA: ABC-CLIO, 2008.

Fredriksen, John C. *American Military Leaders: From Colonial Times to the Present.* 2 vols. Santa Barbara, CA: ABC-CLIO, 1999.

Fredriksen, John C. *America's Military Adversaries: From Colonial Times to the Present.* Santa Barbara, CA: ABC-CLIO, 2001.

Freeman, Douglas Southall. *Lee's Lieutenants: A Study in Command.* New York: Simon & Schuster, 2001.

Garrison, Webb. *Amazing Women of the Civil War: Fascinating True Stories of Women Who Made a Difference.* Nashville, TN: Thomas Nelson, 1999.

Genovese, Michael A. *Encyclopedia of the American Presidency* (rev. ed.). New York: Infobase, 2008.

Gillis, Jennifer Blizin. *Robert E. Lee: Confederate Commander*. North Mankato, MN: Capstone, 2005.

Graf, John F. *Standard Catalog of Civil War Firearms*. Iola, WI: Krause, 2008.

Grant, Ulysses S. *Personal Memoirs of Ulysses S. Grant*. New York: Cosimo, 2007.

Grimsley, Mark. *And Keep Moving On: The Virginia Campaign, May–June 1864*. Lincoln: University of Nebraska Press, 2002.

Hacker, J. David. "A Census-Based Count of the Civil War Dead." *Civil War History* 57, no. 4 (December 2011): 307–48.

Hakim, Joy. *A History of US*. Book Six: *War, Terrible War*. New York: Oxford University Press, 2005.

Hale, Donald R. *They Called Him Bloody Bill: The Life of William Anderson, Missouri Guerilla*. Clinton, MO: The Printery, 1992.

Harper, Judith E. *Women During the Civil War: An Encyclopedia*. New York: Taylor & Francis, 2004.

Harrell, Roger Herman. *The 2nd North Carolina Cavalry*. Jefferson, NC: McFarland, 2004.

Hazlett, James C., Edwin Olmstead, and M. Hume Parks. *Field Artillery Weapons of the Civil War* (rev. ed.). Champaign: University of Illinois Press, 2004.

Heidler, David S., and Jeanne T. Heidler, eds. *Encyclopedia of the American Civil War: A Political, Social, and Military History*. New York: W. W. Norton, 2002.

Hewitt, Lawrence Lee, and Arthur W. Bergeron Jr. *Confederate Generals in the Western Theater: Classic Essays on America's Civil War*. 3 vols. Knoxville: University of Tennessee Press, 2010, 2011, and 2013.

Higginson, Thomas Wentworth. *Army Life in a Black Regiment*. Boston: Fields, Osgood, & Co., 1870.

Howard, Blair. *Battlefields of the Civil War: A Guide for Travellers*. West Palm Beach, FL: Hunter, 2007.

Johnson, Curt, and Mark McLaughlin. *Civil War Battles*. Reprint, New York: Fairfax, 1981.

Johnson, David Alan. *Decided on the Battlefield: Grant, Sherman, Lincoln and the Election of 1864*. Amherst, NY: Prometheus, 2012.

Jones, Terry L. *Historical Dictionary of the Civil War*. 2nd ed. 2 vols. Lanham, MD: Scarecrow, 2011.

Jones, Terry L. "The Terrifying Tigers." *The New York Times* (online). September 13, 2011. opinionator.blogs.nytimes.com/2011/09/13/the-terrifying-tigers.

Jones, Wilmer L. *Generals in Blue and Gray*. 2 vols. Mechanicsburg, PA: Stackpole Books, 2006.

Jordan, Brian Matthew. *Unholy Sabbath: The Battle of South Mountain in History and Memory, September 14, 1862*. New York: Savas Beatie, 2012.

Jordan, Ervin L., Jr., and Herbert A. Thomas Jr. *19th Virginia Infantry*. Lynchburg, VA: H. E. Howard, 1987.

Katcher, Philip R. N. *Flags of the American Civil War*. Oxford, UK: Osprey, 1993.

Kelly, C. Brian. *Best Little Stories from the Civil War: More Than 100 True Stories*. Nashville, TN: Cumberland House, 1998.

Kennedy, Frances H. *The Civil War Battlefield Guide*. 2nd ed. Boston: Houghton Mifflin, 1998.

Kershaw, W. L. *History of Page County Iowa: Also Biographical Sketches of Some Prominent Citizens of the County*. Chicago: S. J. Clarke, 1909.

Kessel, William B., and Robert Wooster. *Encyclopedia of Native American Wars and Warfare*. New York: Infobase, 2005.

Kinard, Jeff. *Pistols: An Illustrated History of Their Impact*. Santa Barbara, CA: ABC-CLIO, 2003.

Konstam, Angus. *The Pocket Book of Civil War Weapons: From Small Arms to Siege Artillery*. London: Salamander, 2004.

Lanning, Michael Lee. *The Civil War 100: The Stories Behind the Most Influential Battles, People and Events in the War Between the States*. Naperville, IL: Sourcebooks, 2007.

Linedecker, Clifford L., ed. *Civil War, A to Z: The Complete Handbook of America's Bloodiest Conflict*. New York: Random House, 2007.

MacDonald, John. *Great Battlefields of the World*. New York: Collier Books, 1985.

MacDonald, John. *Great Battles of the Civil War*. New York: Collier Books, 1988.

Martinez, J. Michael. *Carpetbaggers, Cavalry, and the Ku Klux Klan: Exposing the Invisible Empire During Reconstruction*. Lanham, MD: Rowman & Littlefield, 2007.

McKenna, Joseph. *British Ships in the Confederate Navy*. Jefferson, NC: McFarland, 2010.

McLachlan, Sean. *American Civil War Guerilla Tactics*. Oxford, UK: Osprey, 2009.

McNeese, Tim. *America's Civil War*. Dayton, OH: Lorenz Educational Press, 2003.

McPherson, James M. *Battle Cry of Freedom: The Civil War Era*. (Oxford History of the United States). New York: Oxford University Press, 2003.

Metz, Leon Claire. *The Encyclopedia of Lawmen, Outlaws, and Gunfighters*. New York: Infobase, 2003.

Miles, Rosalind, and Robin Cross. *Hell Hath No Fury: True Stories of Women at War from Antiquity to Iraq*. New York: Three Rivers Press, 2008.

Moller, George D. *American Military Shoulder Arms*. Albuquerque: University Press of New Mexico, 2011.

Morelock, J. D. *The Army Times Book of Great Land Battles: From the Civil War to the Gulf War*. New York: Berkley Books, 1999.

Mountjoy, Shane, and Tim McNeese, consulting ed. *Technology and the Civil War*. New York: Infobase, 2009.

Mowery, David L. *Morgan's Great Raid: The Remarkable Expedition from Kentucky to Ohio.* Charleston, SC: The History Press, 2013.

National Park Service. *The Civil War.* nps.gov/civilwar.

Nicholas, Richard L., and Joseph Servis. *Powhatan, Salem and Courtney Henrico Artillery.* Lynchburg, VA: H. E. Howard, Inc., 1997.

Nofi, Albert A. *A Civil War Treasury: Being a Miscellany of Arms and Artillery, Facts and Figures, Legends and Lore, Muses and Minstrels, Personalities and People.* Cambridge, MA: Da Capo, 1995.

Oliphant, William James. Edited by James M. McCaffrey. *Only a Private: A Texan Remembers the Civil War: The Memoirs of William J. Oliphant.* Houston, TX: Halcyon Press, 2004.

Perrett, Bryan. *At All Costs! Stories of Impossible Victories.* London: Arms and Armour, 1993.

Poole, Robert M. *On Hallowed Ground: The Story of Arlington National Cemetery.* New York: Bloomsbury, 2009.

Power, J. Tracy. "Brother Against Brother: Alexander and James Campbell's Civil War," *South Carolina Historical Magazine* 95, no. 2 (April 1994): 130–41.

Pritchard, Russ A., Jr. *Raiders of the Civil War: Untold Stories of Actions Behind the Lines.* Guilford, CT: Globe Pequot, 2005.

Pryor, Elizabeth Brown. *Reading the Man: A Portrait of Robert E. Lee Through His Private Letters.* New York: Viking, 2007.

Rawley, James A. *Turning Points of the Civil War.* Reprint, Lincoln: University of Nebraska Press, 1989.

Reef, Catherine. *African Americans in the Military* (rev. ed.). New York: Infobase, 2010.

Rhea, Gordon C. *The Battles for Spotsylvania Court House and the Road to Yellow Tavern, May 7–12, 1864.* Baton Rouge: Louisiana State University Press, 1997.

Ridley, Bromfield L. *Battles and Sketches of the Army of Tennessee.* Mexico, MO: Missouri Printing & Publishing, 1906.

Rottman, Gordon L. *The Most Daring Raid of the Civil War: The Great Locomotive Chase.* New York: Rosen, 2011.

Sandler, Stanley L., ed.; Michael Ashkenazi, and Paul D. Buell, associate eds. *Ground Warfare: An International Encyclopedia.* 3 vols. Santa Barbara, CA: ABC-CLIO, 2002.

Schreckengost, Gary. "1st Louisiana Special Battalion at the Battle of Manassas." *America's Civil War Magazine* 12, no. 2 (May 1999).

Schreckengost, Gary. *The First Louisiana Special Battalion: Wheat's Tigers in the Civil War.* Jefferson, NC: McFarland, 2008.

Schroeder-Lein, Glenna R. *The Encyclopedia of Civil War Medicine.* Armonk, NY: M. E. Sharpe, 2008.

Sears, Stephen W. *Gettysburg.* Boston: Houghton Mifflin, 2004.

Shearer, Benjamin F., ed. *Home Front Heroes: A Biographical Dictionary of Americans During Wartime*. 3 vols. Westport, CT: Greenwood, 2007.

Sheridan, Robert E. *Iron from the Deep: The Discovery and Recovery of the USS Monitor*. Annapolis, MD: Naval Institute Press, 2004.

Sherman, William T. *Memoirs of General William Tecumseh Sherman*. Edited and with an introduction and notes by Michael Fellman. New York: Penguin Books, 2000.

Sifakis, Stewart. *Compendium of the Confederate Armies*. 11 vols. New York: Facts on File, 1992–1995.

Silverstone, Paul H. *Civil War Navies, 1855–1883*. 5 vols. Boca Raton, FL: CRC Press, 2006.

Sinclair, Arthur. *Two Years on the* Alabama. Charleston, SC: Nabu Press, 2010.

Smith, Robin. *American Civil War Zouaves*. Illustrated by Bill Younghusband. Oxford, UK: Osprey, 1996.

Stern, Philip Van Doren. *The Confederate Navy: A Pictorial History*. Garden City, NY: Doubleday, 1962.

Sutherland, Jonathan D. *African Americans at War: An Encyclopedia*. 2 vols. Santa Barbara, CA: ABC-CLIO, 2004.

Symonds, Craig L. *The Civil War at Sea*. Reprint, New York: Oxford University Press, 2012.

The Civil War. Film directed by Ken Burns. Narrated by David McCullough et al. 5 episodes. Arlington, VA: PBS. Aired Sept. 23–27, 1990.

The Civil War Society's Encyclopedia of the Civil War: The Complete and Comprehensive Guide to the American Civil War. New York: Wings Books, 1997.

Thomas, Emory M. *Robert E. Lee: A Biography*. New York: W. W. Norton, 1997.

Trudeau, Noah Andre. *Gettysburg: A Testing of Courage*. New York: HarperCollins, 2002.

Tucker, Spencer C. *Almanac of American Military History*. 4 vols. Santa Barbara, CA: ABC-CLIO, 2012.

Tucker, Spencer C., ed.; Paul G. Pierpaoli, associate ed.; and William E. White III, assistant ed. *The Civil War Naval Encyclopedia*. 2 vols. Santa Barbara, CA: ABC-CLIO, 2011.

Underwood, Rodman L. *Waters of Discord: The Union Blockade of Texas During the Civil War*. Jefferson, NC: McFarland, 2008.

Velazquez, Loreta Janeta. *The Woman in Battle: The Civil War Narrative of Loreta Janeta Velazquez, Cuban Woman and Confederate Soldier*. Madison: University of Wisconsin Press, 2003.

Wagner, Heather Lehr, and Tim McNeese, consulting ed. *Spies in the Civil War*. New York: Infobase, 2009.

Wagner, Margaret E., Gary W. Gallagher, and Paul Finkelman, eds. Foreword by

James M. McPherson. *The Library of Congress Civil War Desk Reference*. Reprint, New York: Simon & Schuster, 2009.

Ward, Andrew. *River Run Red: The Fort Pillow Massacre in the American Civil War*. New York: Penguin Books, 2005.

Weir, William. *50 Military Leaders Who Changed the World*. Franklin Lakes, NJ: New Page Books, 2007.

Welker, David A. *Tempest at Ox Hill: The Battle of Chantilly*. Cambridge, MA: Da Capo Press, 2002.

Wilbur, C. Keith. *Civil War Medicine 1861–1865*. Guilford, CT: Globe Pequot, 1998.

Willbanks, James H., ed. *America's Heroes: Medal of Honor Recipients from the Civil War to Afghanistan*. Santa Barbara, CA: ABC-CLIO, 2011.

Wills, Brian Steel. *The Confederacy's Greatest Cavalryman: Nathan Bedford Forrest*. Lawrence: University Press of Kansas, 1998.

Wilson, John Alfred. *Adventures of Alf. Wilson: A Thrilling Episode of the Dark Days of the Rebellion*. Toledo, OH: Blade Printing, 1880.

Wilson, Walter E., and Gary L. McKay. *James D. Bulloch: Secret Agent and Mastermind of the Confederate Navy*. Jefferson, NC: McFarland, 2012.

Worden, John L., Samuel D. Greene, and H. Ashton Ramsay. *The* Monitor *and the* Merrimac: *Both Sides of the Story*. New York: Harper, 1912.

Wyeth, John Allan. *That Devil Forrest: Life of General Nathan Bedford Forrest*. Baton Rouge: Louisiana State University Press, 1989.

Yi Sun-sin. *Nanjung Ilgi: War Diary of Admiral Yi Sun-sin*. Edited by Sohn Powkey. Translated by Ha Tae-hung. Seoul, South Korea: Yonsei University Press, 1980.

Index

⭐ ⭐ ⭐

DID YOU KNOW...

...the Vikings believed that the sound of thunder comes from the god Thor clubbing Frost Giants with his giant hammer Mjölnir?

...Danish king Harald Wartooth's army included a unit of three hundred ferocious warrior women known as shield-maidens?

...a Viking hero named Ragnar supposedly got the awesome nickname "Hairy Breeches" when he rescued a princess from a giant serpent by fashioning snake-proof armor out of hair and tar?

LOOK FOR ALL THESE STORIES AND MORE IN
GUTS & GLORY: THE VIKINGS

AVAILABLE MAY 2015

TURN THE PAGE FOR A PREVIEW!

The Viking Warrior

The tactics, equipment, and ferocious might that terrorized the world for over two centuries

793–1066 AD

> Odin could make his enemies in battle blind, or deaf, or terror-struck, and their weapons so blunt that they could no more cut than a willow wand; on the other hand, his men rushed forwards without armor, were as mad as dogs or wolves, bit their shields, and were as strong as bears or wild bulls, and killed people at a blow, but neither fire nor iron told upon themselves. These were called Berserker.
>
> —Snorri Sturluson, *Ynglinga Saga*

FROM IRELAND TO RUSSIA, PARIS TO CONstantinople, and everywhere in between, there was no more terrifying sight than a war band of gigantic Viking marauders clambering over the sides of their longships, crashing down into the ankle-deep surf, and charging forward with their armor shining in the sunlight, their axes and swords raised fearsomely above their heads. Although known by nearly a dozen different names—Northmen, Ashmen, Norsemen, Danes, Varangians, the Norse, and others—the people we now know as Vikings stood for hundreds of years as a symbol of ruin and destruction, throughout the period of European history known as the Dark Ages. They were an unstoppable force that struck paralyzing fear into the hearts of all, from the lowliest peasants to the most heavily armored knights.

Vikings typically weren't professional warriors and raiders. Ravaging thatched-roof cottages with torches and steel was just something they did as a fun hobby and a way to make some extra cash in the summer. Family men, brothers, fathers, and sons, the Vikings came from all walks of life across Scandinavia—the regions of present-day Norway, Sweden, and Denmark. They embarked on their raiding expeditions for a variety of reasons ranging from glory, adventure, and wealth to the necessity of putting food on their tables during the long, cold Arctic winters. The only requirement was that each warrior had to provide his own gear.

In the early days of the Viking Age, the Northmen weren't organized into kingdoms and countries the way we think of them today. Their lands were really just a mishmash of minor dominions, each ruled by a guy known as a jarl. The jarls were each responsible for recruiting their own men from their lands and putting together their own raiding parties; they did whatever they felt like without having to report to anyone in particular.

A jarl (sometimes they called themselves kings) would have a small bodyguard of professional warriors known as a *hird*. A jarl's *hird* would be made up of *hersir*, minor nobles who served him. The *hersir* would have all the best gear, get the most plunder, and join the jarl on raids and adventures. Below the *hersir* were freemen—landowners, farmers, and craftsmen. The freemen could join on as Vikings if they wanted, but they were required to serve in the jarl's levies, meaning that if the jarl was attacked by a rival gang of Viking warriors (something that happened more frequently than you might think), the freemen had to grab their spears and shields and defend their homes. At the bottom of the pecking order were the thralls—the slaves. Thralls had no rights and could be killed or sacrificed at their master's command, but if they had a good master, there was a chance he'd let them buy or win their freedom. In a pinch, a thrall could be given a weapon and allowed to fight, but most Vikings didn't trust them enough to let that happen.

Although Viking gear varied wildly depending on how much the warrior was willing to spend on it, the typical Norseman's primary weapon was a spear. He would carry two—a light javelin for throwing and a heavy spear for stabbing. The javelin had a barbed tip so it would stick into enemy shields, rendering them useless, and it was made of lightweight steel that would bend when it hit something, which prevented the enemy from throwing your own javelin back at you. The heavy spear was made of ash wood, stood six to eight feet high, and could be wielded in one hand, leaving the other hand free to hold the shield.

There were also two types of axes—the short axe, which was the perfect size for hiding behind the shield, and the much-feared Danish long axe: a gigantic six-foot-long, two-handed battle-axe with a single twelve-inch blade. It could cut through armor, horses, and men alike with one swing, shredding shields and splitting helmets like a chain saw through warm butter. The only downside to this weapon was that a warrior couldn't carry a shield with it, but the axe made up for it with sheer firepower. On more than one occasion, the Norse sagas refer to Vikings cutting through two and even three enemies with a single swing of the weapon.

Swords were an extraordinarily expensive item carried only by the richest Vikings, and were by far the most treasured weapon in the Viking arsenal. Given cool names like Gold-Hilt, Leg-Biter, and Long-and-Sharp, these double-edged straight blades were forged of iron, and their hilts were decorated in gold and silver and souped up with protective runes, healing stones, or bone fragments from animals or long-dead heroes. The legendary sword Skofnung, carried by King Hrolf Kraki, was said to be imbued with the spirits of twelve great heroes and would allegedly "sing" when it made contact with the enemy.

A long, single-bladed knife called a sax rounded out the Viking arsenal. Some Vikings also carried bows, but even though all Norsemen could shoot well enough to hunt, they considered arrows a "coward's weapon" and far preferred to throw spears and rocks at their enemies or kill them face-to-face the old-fashioned way. (It's worth mentioning, however, that the Norse did have great respect for the Finns, who could ski downhill and accurately shoot arrows at the same time.)

To defend themselves from their enemies, the Vikings wore armor fashioned from leather, bone, quilted fabric, or animal hide, and a helmet typically of the same material. *Hersir* warriors could sometimes afford imposing chain mail shirts that weighed in at about twenty-six pounds, as well as cool-looking metal helmets with eye and nose protection. But no matter how hard TV might try to convince you, real Viking helmets didn't have horns on them. That touch was actually added by German opera costumers in the nineteenth century.

Finally, Vikings carried a brightly painted round shield made of wood, with a sturdy metal disk in the center to protect their hands. The shields were light and easy to carry and could be worn on the back, but they wouldn't survive more than a few battles before needing to be replaced.

One group of guys who needed to replace their shields

more often than everyone else was the terrifying *berserkir*, a group we know in English as the berserkers. Taking their name from the Norse word for "bear shirts," berserkers were a small, elite group of vicious, unruly warriors who went into battle completely naked except for a he-man-style loincloth and the pelt of either a wolf or a bear worn over their shoulders like a superhero's cape. These terrifying fighters howled and growled like animals and got so pumped up before battles that they would bite big chunks out of their shields before they attacked. Part of a mysterious cult dedicated to the god Odin, berserkers would prepare for battle the night before, sitting around a campfire drinking mysterious concoctions and working themselves up into an over-the-top rabid battle frenzy. Believing themselves to be possessed by Odin and the spirits of the animals whose pelts they wore, by the time battle began the next day, the berserkers would be frothing at the mouth like madmen, utterly freaking out anyone who saw them. They would always be the first to charge into battle. The phrase "going berserk" comes from these guys. They were almost completely immune to physical pain of any kind. Occasionally, they could be found in intense hand-to-hand combat with trees, rocks, and other inanimate objects hours after the actual battle had ended.

But most semi-sane Vikings didn't actually want to encounter the enemy on the field of battle. These guys much preferred plundering and raiding to out-and-out combat.

There was a much smaller chance of being impaled when you were fighting disorganized peasants with pitchforks and rakes than when you were facing heavily armored royal cavalry that were packing lances and shields. When big-time, organized military battles did break out, the Vikings weren't just a horde of undisciplined wild men—they locked themselves into battle formation using a tactic known as the shield wall. A fairly common strategy in medieval times, the shield wall was basically a big line of guys who would interlock their shields, run at the enemy, and then stab with their spears to break the enemy's formation. Once the enemy line was broken, a second line of Viking axemen and swordmen would rush into the gap and start swinging for the fences. In large-scale battles, the Vikings lost about as many as they won—which is probably why they tried to avoid them.

Women did accompany the Vikings on their raids, but despite a few stories of hardcore warrior women known as shield-maidens raiding and fighting on the high seas, they mostly served as cooks, nurses, and healers. In addition to treating all the weird diseases that were pervasive throughout the Middle Ages (like leprosy, tuberculosis, and malaria), women would patch up wounds, treat infections, repair broken gear, and diagnose everything from blood poisoning to tetanus. They would reset broken bones, amputate limbs when necessary, cut out arrowheads, and cauterize and sew up badly bleeding injuries, first salting the wound to numb it, then sealing it by touching it with a red-hot poker, and finally stitching it up with thread. Sometimes a woman would be both cook and nurse. A typical after-battle feast was a gross-tasting soup made up of little more than onions and garlic. The next morning, the women would smell the stomachs of men who had been stabbed in the torso—if they could smell the garlic, it meant the man's stomach had been cut open, and nothing could be done to save him. He'd simply be left behind to die.

But that's the life of a Viking warrior for you. For many, all that awaited was a cruel, unceremonious, painful death alone in a hostile foreign land. But for those who made it through the dangers of Viking life, the promise of untold wealth and glory awaited. Poets were ready to sing the battle deeds of brave warriors and come up with epic nicknames for them to be remembered by. Gold and silver were sitting there for the taking from the wealthiest lands in Europe, and massive fame and fortune awaited all those who sought glory over long life.

Warriors and . . . Poets?

Viking deeds of heroic greatness were recounted by Norse war-rior-poets known as skalds, many of whom were just as efficient with a pen as they were with a broadsword. Known for its flowery depictions of incredibly brutal events, skaldic verse uses idioms, metaphors, and phrases called kenning that add a whole other layer of awesomeness to the writing. For instance, instead of saying "blood," a skald might say "corpse beer," "dew of slaughter," or "battle sweat." Death becomes "the sword's sleep." Ships are "sea-steeds," and battle is "the sword quarrel" or "weapon storm." Some of it makes sense, and some of it—like "Northern kiss" for a cold wind, or "ship of night" for the moon—can be really confusing. But how can you not like literature that reads like lyrics on a heavy metal album and changes "The king's men won the battle" to something like "The ring giver's children of battle weathered the weapon storm"? The guitar riff writes itself.

What's in a Name?

Tons of great Viking nicknames pop up throughout the sagas. Among my personal favorites are Haldar the Unchristian, Thord Horse-Head, Thorfinn Skull-Cleaver, Thorleif Goti the Overbearing, Hrolf the Woman-Loving, Odd the Wide-Traveling, Sven Reaper, Harald Wartooth, Hadd the Hard, Olaf the Peacock, Erik the Priest-Hater, Einar Jingle-Scale, and Eyvind the Plagiarist. Most of these were proud nicknames for brave fighters, but this wasn't always the case—one Viking raider was mockingly nicknamed "the Children's Man," as a way of making fun of him because he once stopped another Viking from knocking over a baby's crib.

Ulfbehrt Steel

The quality of Viking-era blades varied wildly, but the best by far was Ulfbehrt steel. Forged at a mysterious smithy in Frankland (present-day France and Germany), Ulfbehrt blades were wildly expensive and were carried only by the elite of the Viking world. Almost a thousand years before its time, Ulfbehrts were made with crucible steel, an incredibly pure steel not produced in Europe until the 1700s. Nobody knows who Ulfbehrt is or where he got his steel (some theorize he imported it from the Middle East through the Volga trade route with Russia), but his blades were flexible, wouldn't break in battle, kept their edge, and punched through any armor the Middle Ages had to offer. Ulfbehrt steel was so highly regarded that lesser smithies actually started producing cheap knockoffs to make a quick buck.

The Prequel

Even though Lindisfarne, a small island off the northeast coast of England, is listed as the site of the first great Viking raid in Britain and the official beginning of the Viking Age, the first Viking longships actually appeared off the coast four years earlier. In 789, three ships rolled into the harbor of Portland, on the southwest coast of England, sailing up to the dock to check things out. The English harbormaster headed down to collect their docking fee, but the Vikings killed him with a spear, pushed off, and got out of there without paying their parking ticket. Some historians like to say this was the first real Viking raid in Europe, but it hardly counts.

The World in 800 AD

One of the biggest pains in the butt about Viking history is that a lot of the places and peoples the Vikings ran into don't really exist anymore. For instance, modern-day England was actually four different countries in 800 AD, and France and Germany were squished together into one big kingdom. China was still China, but almost the entire Middle East was ruled by one guy, Russia was made up of a hundred different little tribes, and nobody had even heard of North America because a lot of Europeans thought if you sailed west from Spain, you'd fall off the end of the earth and be eaten by a sea monster. It's annoying.

Well, to help out, here's a primer on some of the names and places that might have appeared on the map if a Viking war leader could have pulled up a GPS on his cell phone.

Tang Dynasty China

At this time, Eastern Asia was completely dominated by the unstoppable might of China. Led by the far-reaching emperors of the Tang Dynasty, China was the richest kingdom on earth and was in the middle of a golden age of learning, art, and music. Buddhist monks were worshiping in towering pagodas and monasteries; caravans loaded with gold, silks, and exotic goods were making their way up and down the famous Silk Road, which connected China to the Middle East; and Chinese scientists were inventing things like playing cards, government bureaucracy, and gunpowder, which they used mostly for fireworks and handheld flame-throwers. Sure, the emperor Xuanzong had a few rebellions and barbarian uprisings to deal with, but that's par for the course when you're talking about imperial China.

Over in Korea, the Kingdom of Silla was enjoying a cultural and economic happy fun time of its own, and in Southeast Asia the Khmer Empire was beginning to think about construction of an amazing, sprawling stone temple complex known as Angkor Wat. Just off the coast, Japan was entering the Nara period. A powerful emperor had just moved the capital to Kyoto, and scholars were using the newly adopted Chinese system of writing to create impressive works of literature and poetry.

The Maya

North America hadn't been discovered yet, but that didn't mean there weren't people living there and doing cool things. The really big deals in the New World in the 800s were the Maya, who were building towering, pyramid-like limestone structures, making incredible advances in astronomy and mathematics, decorating their cities with the bleached skulls of their defeated enemies, and playing that cool-looking basketball game where the hoop is turned sideways and you can only hit the ball with your elbows or knees.

The Byzantine Empire

All of eastern Europe was controlled by the Byzantine Empire, a Roman dynasty run by a Greek emperor who lived in what is now the biggest city in Turkey. Confused yet?

Around 330 AD, the once-powerful Roman Empire split in half, fracturing into the Western Roman Empire, based in Rome, and the Eastern Roman Empire, based in the incredibly wealthy fortress city of Constantinople, in what used to be Greece. The Western Empire was overrun by barbarians in 410 and completely fell apart, but Constantinople managed to fight off hordes of barbarian attackers from every direction and eventually grew into the richest and most dominant empire in Europe. Sitting on a golden throne behind the impenetrable triple walls of his mighty city, the Byzantine emperor ruled over millions of subjects and commanded absolute obedience from a mighty army that included everything from mercenary barbarian warriors to battle-hardened Greek armored troops.

The Abbasid Caliphate

The Islamic world was ruled by a guy known as the caliph, who was like a king, only he had a lot of religious power as well. His realm, known as the caliphate, was based in Baghdad, Iraq, and at this time dominated a huge swath of land stretching from the borders of the Byzantine Empire all the way down through North Africa. The Abbasid caliph had just taken control of the Muslim world from a rival dynasty known as the Umayyads in a bloody coup a few years earlier. (The Umayyads still held a stronghold in Spain, which bugged the Abbasids, but they couldn't really do anything about it.) All across the Muslim world a golden age was blossoming, with huge steps taken in architecture, mathematics, medicine, literature, and science. Muslim scholars and scientists built towering mosques, ornate libraries, observatories, and universities, began mass-producing paper for the first time, created calculus, and even invented the number zero, which I guess wasn't around until this point.

The British Isles

England, by comparison, was still basically in the Dark Ages. Far from being one unified Great Britain, England was divided up into four rival kingdoms, each with some little king involved in his own annoying infighting against the other three. Ireland and Scotland were loose groups of Gaelic and Celtic clans without any overarching direction or central power structure, which made them easy targets for Viking marauders.

The Frankish Kingdom

On mainland Europe, the Vikings faced a hardcore enemy in 800 AD. The lands of present-day France, Germany, Belgium, Switzerland, and the Netherlands were known as the Frankish Kingdom and were ruled by the mighty emperor Charlemagne—a big, scary German warrior-king who had forged a Christian empire by marching on the barbarian tribes of Europe and unifying them by killing anyone who refused to be baptized Catholic. With the backing of the pope in Rome, Charlemagne solidified his rule with an iron fist, creating one of the most powerful empires mainland Europe had ever seen.

Charlemagne had his first encounter with the Northmen in the year 799, when a small band of Viking sea-raiders attacked a settlement on the northern coast of present-day France. The ruler of the Franks didn't hesitate to move on this threat. He was a man of action, and he immediately ordered that huge fleets of warships be positioned at the entrances of every major trade river that bordered the North Sea. Vikings attempted a few small raids on his territory but were quickly turned away by stalwart lines of imperial warships and fire-tipped arrows. The Danes never gained a foothold in Charlemagne's domain as long as he lived, but when he died in 814 AD, he passed his empire to his son Louis the Pious, who ultimately made a terrible mistake by dividing the Frankish Empire into three smaller kingdoms and giving one to each of his sons. Louis had hoped that this would keep his sons from killing each other in wars of succession that would break his hard-won empire apart. It didn't work.

The sons of Louis the Pious went to war immediately, each trying to destroy the others and reunite Charlemagne's empire for themselves. They took all the fleets, warships, gold, and soldiers amassed through decades of prosperity and turned them on one another in a petty blood feud for power.

The road was now open for the Vikings to do their thing.

They attacked without mercy. The once-prosperous port city of Dorestad was sacked four times in four years, from 834 to 837. The former capital at Rouen was laid waste. The Rhine, Loire, and Seine Rivers were plundered ruthlessly, with Vikings killing bishops, burning towns, grabbing slaves, looting, destroying, and leaving nothing but smoldering embers in their wake. In 845, a Viking called Ragnar Hairy Breeches defeated an imperial force and sacked Paris, stripping the outer ring of the city of its valuables before accepting payment of seven thousand pounds of silver to leave. Flanders, the Rhineland, and Picardy, almost completely undefended, were ravaged. Charles the Bald, one of Louis's sons and now emperor of the Western Frankish Kingdom (basically modern-day France), was so caught up in his own petty arguments that he did nothing, offering payments to Viking leaders in 858, 863, 866, and 867 just to leave him alone. Little did he know this was just the beginning of what the Vikings would have in store.